DON'T
LOOK
AWAY!

Snapshots of Congo and
the Pygmies of Mubambiro

BARBARA ROSE FERGUSON

a. Acorn
Press

Published by Acorn Press
An imprint of Bible Society Australia
ACN 148 058 306 | Charity licence 19 000 528
GPO Box 4161
Sydney NSW 2001
Australia
www.acornpress.net.au | www.biblesociety.org.au

ISBN 978-0-647-53353-6

First published by Morning Star Publishing in 2019,
ISBN 978-1-648-45389-5

NATIONAL
LIBRARY
OF AUSTRALIA

A catalogue record for this
work is available from the
National Library of Australia

Cover and text design and layout by John Healy

In memory of the people of the forest on Mount Shove,
Democratic Republic of the Congo

CONTENTS

Acknowledgements

My sincere thanks to all my friends and supporters who encouraged me in the writing of this account of my experiences in Congo. Special thanks to David and Heather Kelly, who read the first draft and made many helpful comments and suggestions based on their own many trip to Goma.

I am so grateful to Sue Harvey, surely the best of editors, from whose careful, insightful editing I've learnt so much about writing.

I could never have had these experiences to record without the team of people in Congo who have guarded and guided me through the past ten years – especially Virginie, Samuel, Fabien, Thomson and Martin – and of course Dr Jo Lusi at HEAL Africa Hospital, without whose support I would never have got into the country.

I don't pretend to be an expert on Pygmies or on the Democratic Republic of the Congo. What I've said in this book is based on what I've seen and heard in the course of my work. Inevitably, sometimes I will have misunderstood or misinterpreted. I take full responsibility for all errors and apologise sincerely if I have offended anyone in any way.

Most of all I acknowledge the people of the forest, displaced from Mount Shove and still struggling to survive in a hostile environment. They are all precious to me and I thank them for letting me into their lives, forgiving me my mistakes and trusting me to have their best interests at heart.

Abbreviations

ADRA	Seventh Day Adventist Rural Development Agency
AIDS	Acquired Immune Deficiency Syndrome
BITS	Brief Intervention for Trauma Survivors
CNDP	National Congress for the Defence of the People
FDLR	Democratic Forces for the Liberation of Rwanda
GDG	Global Development Group
HAH	HEAL Africa Hospital
HIV	Human Immunodeficiency Virus
MONUSCO	United Nations Organization Stabilization Mission in the Democratic Republic of the Congo
NGO	Non-governmental organisation
PCC	Pygmy Child Care
UN	United Nations

Swahili words

Amani	peace
Asante	thanks
Barabara	highway
Bambuti	Pygmies (pl.)
Bantu	People (pl.)
Chukudus	unique-to-Congo wheelbarrow/scooters
Fufu	staple food made with cassava flour
Hapana	no
Kanga	piece of material for a wrap-around skirt
Mai Mai	illegal local civilian defence force
Mali	bride price
Mbuti	Pygmy (sing.)
Mubarikiwe	be blessed (pl.)
Mzungu	foreigner
Mzee	old
Ndiyo	yes
Ntu	person
Ubarikiwe	be blessed (sing.)

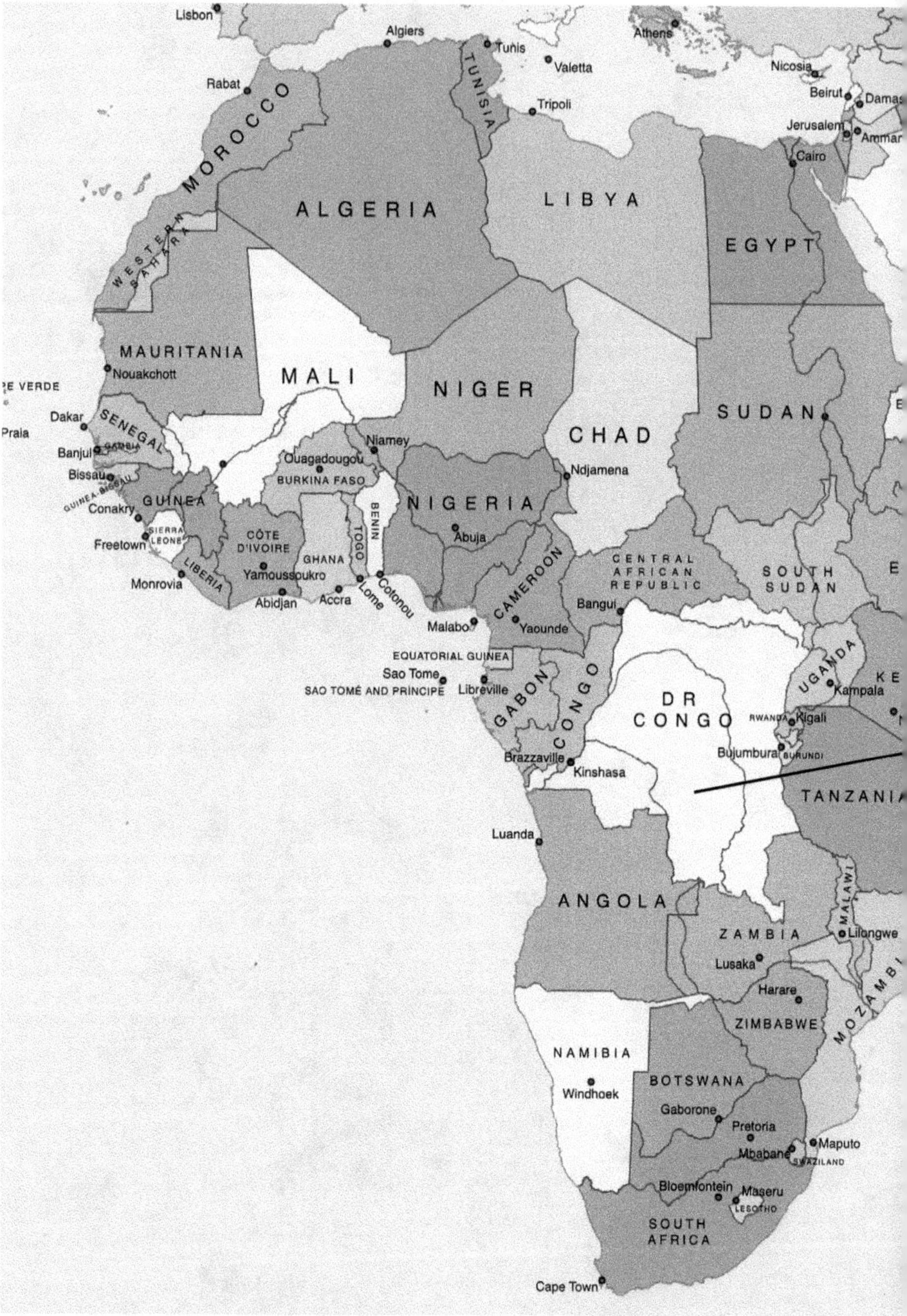

Lisbon
Algiers
Tunis
Athens
Valetta
Nicosia
Rabat
Beirut
Tripoli
Jerusalem
Cairo
MOROCCO
TUNISIA
ALGERIA
LIBYA
EGYPT
WESTERN SAHARA
MAURITANIA
Nouakchott
MALI
NIGER
SUDAN
Dakar
Praia
SENEGAL
Banjul
GAMBIA
CHAD
Niamey
Ouagadougou
BURKINA FASO
Bissau
GUINEA-BISSAU
GUINEA
Ndjamena
Conakry
NIGERIA
BENIN
TOGO
SIERRA LEONE
Freetown
CÔTE D'IVOIRE
Abuja
GHANA
Yamoussoukro
LIBERIA
Monrovia
Abidjan
Accra
Lome
Cotonou
CAMEROON
CENTRAL AFRICAN REPUBLIC
SOUTH SUDAN
Bangui
Malabo
Yaounde
EQUATORIAL GUINEA
UGANDA
Sao Tome
SAO TOMÉ AND PRINCIPE
Libreville
GABON
CONGO
Kampala
DR CONGO
RWANDA
Kigali
Bujumbura
BURUNDI
Brazzaville
Kinshasa
Luanda
ANGOLA
MALAWI
ZAMBIA
Lilongwe
Lusaka
Harare
ZIMBABWE
NAMIBIA
Windhoek
BOTSWANA
Gaborone
Pretoria
Maputo
Mbabane
SWAZILAND
Bloemfontein
Maseru
LESOTHO
SOUTH AFRICA
Cape Town

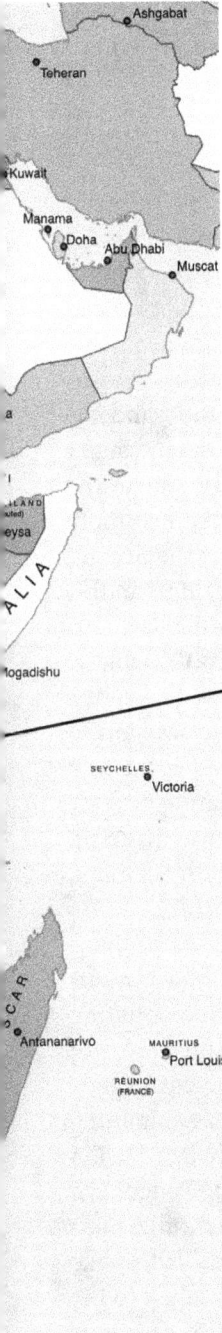

Prologue

'You must read this!' my friend Lesley said as she thrust the weekend edition of the *Sydney Morning Herald* in front of me. 'The world continues to look away. Don't!' ran the big, bold headline above a half-page photo of an African woman trying to conceal her face with a ragged cloth. As I read the text below the photograph I was aghast at the stories of unimaginable brutality being inflicted on tens of thousands of Congolese women. It was 27 November 2007, and in the first six months of the year, four thousand five hundred women had reported violent rape every month – women caught up in a war I'd never heard about. I would soon learn that the war in the Democratic Republic of the Congo (DRC) had in ten years claimed more lives than had been lost in any other country or conflict since the Second World War. The suffering of the women – of all the people caught up in this war – hit me like a body blow. I knew at once that I had to get involved.

I was sixty-seven years old when I read about the plight of the Congolese. My beloved mother, who had been my priority for the past five years, had just died at the age of 101 and I was looking for a new preoccupation to give meaning to my days. Here it was. And the article reminded me of a vow I'd made as an eight-year-old to dedicate my life to alleviating poverty and suffering in Africa. But I'd forgotten about Africa when I was an adult, instead spending eight years as an aid-worker in war-torn South Vietnam, an experience I documented in my first book, *Rain in my Heart*.

Throughout 2008, I met Congolese refugees and other Australians already involved in Congo. I was amazed that although United Nations reports found that Congo's people were enduring the worst humanitarian crisis in the world, this was largely ignored by the international media. I read whatever I could find on Congo's turbulent history and the current tragedy there, and began to understand the many intractable forces maintaining the violence. Then I heard an interview on ABC radio with Lyn Lusi, a woman visiting Australia from North Kivu province in Eastern Congo. Lyn and her husband Jo, an orthopaedic surgeon, had set up the indigenous acute-care HEAL Africa Hospital (HAH) in a city called Goma. Lyn spoke about their efforts to bring physical, spiritual and emotional healing to the thousands of women who came to the hospital with horrendous wounds following rape. Many of these women were infected with HIV, and many were pregnant.

I sent Lyn an email detailing my practical experience with women and children during the war in South Vietnam and the seventeen years I'd spent teaching social work and social development at the University of New South Wales. I asked if I could be of any help in the hospital as a volunteer – perhaps to train staff in strategies to deal with survivors of war and rape trauma. She replied simply, 'Come.'

I've since made eleven trips to Congo, the last in April 2019. Over this time I've continued my association with HAH, which has expanded and developed into a major regional teaching hospital since my first visits. However, on my second visit in 2010 I met a group of Pygmies displaced from their traditional forest homes and living as nomads and beggars in abysmal poverty near the village of Mubambiro, and since then most of my work in both Congo and Australia has revolved around them.

As I write in 2019, the people I know and have come to love in Congo continue to live in ever-present danger of war and disease. The violence goes on, apparently of little interest to the rest of the world. And now, in addition to endemic diseases like typhoid, cholera, measles and malaria, ebola has reached Goma. Ebola is a viral haemorrhagic fever that causes internal bleeding, is highly contagious and was usually fatal until the recent limited availability of a vaccine. I open the inbox on my laptop early every morning and hope that the power and communications systems in Goma will be working so I can receive the latest news from my friends. Their lives are so different from mine, and so difficult. I'm frustrated by the web of complex factors that keep them in miserable circumstances, but thankful that in some cases I've been able to help them or at least offer some comfort and hope.

Last year I came upon that 2007 newspaper report on the suffering in Congo which had so moved me and changed my life. At first I despaired when I realised that many people in that country continue to endure a level of deprivation my fellow Australians can hardly imagine. Subsequently, I went back through the reports I'd written of my work after every visit to Congo and decided that the situation was not as bleak as I'd thought. In each chapter of this book I've used these reports to describe the successes as well as the failures, the highs as well as the lows, of one visit. It is clear that despite the challenges, it has been possible to alleviate the suffering of a small group of this world's most disadvantaged people. While almost certainly the people of the forest can never return from exile to their forest sanctuary on Mount Shove, their children are being given the chance to survive and even thrive in the wider society. I trust that you will not just read about the Pygmies of Mubambiro and forget them. Please – don't look away!

Chapter 1

Do not travel – August 2009

I'm jetlagged, probably dehydrated, both excited and scared. The Australian Government travel advisory website has a clear directive for this region: 'Do not travel.' But here I am in a hired car with a Rwandan driver, approaching the border between the East African nations of Rwanda and Congo. Since flying out of Australia three days ago, I've had three flights with three different airlines and spent four hours on a road still under construction through Rwanda. Now I'm about to enter my final destination: the Congolese frontier city of Goma. For the next month I will work here as a volunteer with staff and rape survivors in the indigenous HEAL Africa Hospital (HAH).

On my way to Nairobi, I had several unsettling misadventures. Somewhere between Sydney and Johannesburg my luggage was broken into and my camera stolen. At Nairobi airport, my pre-paid hotel transport didn't show up, leaving me abandoned after dark at the deserted airport entrance with no taxis in sight. At first I ignored the man loitering at the roadside who kept offering to take me to a hotel. But then I discovered that my mobile phone was locked. Desperately tired, I threw caution to the winds and made a deal with the man to take me to the Serena Hotel. I feared he might take me to a slum, dump me and make off with my bags, but to my relief he drew up at the entrance of a brightly lit compound with lush gardens. We waited at the gates while armed guards ensured there were no bombs under the vehicle – Kenyans are no strangers to terrorist attacks. This man even came into the hotel to support my claim that I'd been stranded at the airport. I was reminded of the random angels who'd come to my rescue when I was an aid-worker in South Vietnam during the war there.

This morning my arrival at Kigali airport in Rwanda was relatively free of drama. I'm now travelling in a vehicle with Deo, the driver used by most volunteers going to the hospital. The road through Rwanda on this last leg of the journey snaked ever higher through the hills, where the soil of the steep slopes on either side of our vehicle was held by thriving Australian eucalyptus trees. Stands of banana trees, corn and cassava fields flashed by. Roadside markets sold live hens and ducks, baskets of eggs, stacks of cabbages, and artfully constructed columns of bright orange carrots. Hollow logs that held beehives for commercial harvesting of honey perched on the upper branches of trees. Ominously, Deo pointed out the ruins of huts that had once housed large families, all now dead, bearing silent witness to the violence of the 1994 genocide. But everywhere at the side of the road, tall, stick-thin people were on the move, on foot or pushing impossibly laden bikes and drays full of produce. The people of Rwanda convey a sense of purpose, and a determination to work their way out of the chaos and poverty of previous years.

Deo slows down and we come to a stop. On our left, between white stucco buildings festooned with red and purple bougainvillea, I glimpse the shining waters of Lake Kivu. I'm feeling increasingly anxious. Although it hasn't been difficult to get visas at the point of arrival in the countries so far, I've been warned it will be different trying to enter Congo. We have no diplomatic missions in Congo and they have none in Australia. I do have a letter of invitation from Dr Jo Lusi, the Director of HAH. Without this, the Rwandan officials could refuse to let me pass into Congo.

It's time to get out of the car, but first I fish out my passport and this precious letter. Deo waves me towards a little one-storey building where people are milling around with documents in hand. I stumble across the rough ground, and yes, I've come to the right window. The official notes the letter and stamps the exit visa in my passport. I follow the other travellers past a sentry box where my documents are checked again, then trundle my luggage behind me across no-man's-land, through boom gates and into Congo.

Instantly I sense a subtle difference about everything here. The sharp rocks underfoot are shiny black lava; the little immigration and customs building is shabby and people make no attempt to form a queue. It's survival of the fittest. People are jostling to get a foothold on the steps in front of the barred window behind which I can see sullen-faced officials. My head thumps –a situation not helped by the press of sweaty bodies and babble of voices in languages I can't understand. A young woman swathed in layers of jewel-coloured cloth tries to push in front of me. Exasperated, I resist. She totters on the narrow step and I'm mortified when I see that, as well as being loaded down with bags of milk and produce she's brought in from Rwanda, she has a small baby secured to her back in a layer of bright cloth.

Incredibly, 'Barbara', I hear my name. Who in this remote place in the heart of Africa knows me? At once I'm embraced by a tiny plump woman with a huge welcoming smile. It's Mama Virginie, public relations officer for HAH with whom I've been corresponding via email for the many months it's taken me to make it to this point. Even with her steering me to the right windows, it seems like ages just to get this simple visa stamp in my passport and pay the close to $500 for a month's stay. Far too much, but I'm not arguing.

At last we're through the formalities, into an HAH vehicle and on our way to Maji Matulivu (Still Waters), the lakeside home of HAH founders Lyn and Jo Lusi, where I'll be staying. In my luggage are all the materials I've prepared for three weeks of training hospital psychosocial counselling staff who work with survivors of rape trauma. I've packed videos of counselling techniques I made with Congolese people in Australia playing the parts, and CDs of the music I'll use to introduce dance therapy. There's lavender oil for aromatherapy and the lecture notes I've had translated into Swahili. This is the culmination of two years of planning for my visit.

***

On the first day at the hospital, I went to the morning chapel service with Samuel, the hospital chaplain assigned to be my interpreter. In Eastern Congo, French and Swahili are the official languages, and not many people speak English. There must have been over a hundred people in the chapel building. The congregation was composed of staff in white coats, and patients, some on crutches, others swathed in bandages. They punctuated the long and impassioned speeches of several leaders with devout cries of 'Amen' or '*Alleluia*'. I couldn't understand a word of the speeches but the *a cappella* singing of the choir of staff and rape survivors was sublime. As we left the chapel, Samuel approached several groups of women and introduced me. I had trouble following the rapid-fire French conversations at first, but soon realised that he was at this late stage trying to recruit staff for my seminars starting the very next day. Finally, he admitted that the two, two-week-long seminars for ten to twelve counsellors that I had planned were now to be one three-week-long training session for any member of staff who turned up. As it happened, twenty-two people enrolled.

Samuel also informed me that he was too busy to be with me every day to translate, and he introduced Zico, his tribal brother, who would be glad of the fee I would pay. I was reluctant to be a burden on the hospital staff, but I thought I really needed a female interpreter. Surely having a male interpreter was entirely inappropriate to discuss the experience of rape with the women! But I was told that apart from Mama Virginie, who had no time to help me, there was no female on the hospital staff who had sufficient English to work with me. So I sat down with Zico to establish a working relationship and discovered his English wasn't too bad. I thought that before we began the workshops we could at least go through the lecture notes that I'd emailed to Samuel several months earlier. Unfortunately, Zico soon told me that the Swahili translation was of the Kenyan variety and wouldn't be clear to the participants, some of whom weren't literate anyway.

The workshops got off to a rocky start. We were at first assigned a room on the upper floor of the hospital administration building, but after the first day the water tank on the roof above burst and flooded the room. We then moved down to a ground-floor room, but a new building was being constructed right next door, and despite the stifling heat, we had to keep the windows closed all day to try to keep out the noise and dust. Challenging conditions for everyone!

The participants were nurses or counsellors who worked in the hospital's various medical departments or the community programs, and some were volunteer counsellors. Several women worked specifically with the gender violence program, others with the program for children living with HIV. One was employed as a literacy teacher for rape survivors and children living in the hospital either with their mothers or because they themselves were having multiple operations. Another participant had a cannula in her arm because twice a day she was receiving intravenous antibiotics for typhoid. I never could be sure exactly who would be present. Time and attendance were flexible, but everyone would turn up for the morning tea and lunch I provided.

When the participants arrived each morning, they scrambled to find a power-point to recharge their mobile phones for free. There are no landlines in Goma, and power, like water, is an unreliable luxury most people can't afford to have installed at home. Roadside entrepreneurs set up a generator and people line up and pay to recharge phones. Outside the university, students can have lecture notes copied at stands where the generator is attached to a photocopier. Even the hospital only has one emergency backup generator during the frequent power cuts that plague this city of a million people. We had a period with power most days, and during these times I played a section of the video on basic counselling techniques for participants. In the discussions after, to my chagrin, it became clear that my volunteer actors in Sydney had improvised as they thought fit, and none of my carefully scripted teaching points were included.

One of the most confident of the counsellors in the workshops allowed me to sit in on her initial meetings with several women so I could understand the nature of her work. We took care to ensure that my presence was as unobtrusive as possible. I could see that her patients' immediate physical needs were being efficiently addressed. But in the workshops, when I watched the role-play of counselling sessions, I could also see that those who played the part of the patients clearly demonstrated symptoms of post-traumatic stress. These exercises led to lively and revealing discussions between me and the participants. I despaired when I learned that despite the best efforts to repair the physical trauma the patients had experienced, most of them would eventually return to the situation where the attacks had occurred and were more than likely in danger of further assault. I wondered how they could possibly get up every day and go on with life with this threat hanging over them.

I felt some concern that my lectures weren't as successful as I'd hoped. More successful were the alternatives to talk therapy I introduced: aromatherapy and dance therapy. Dance therapy to the CDs I'd brought, and would leave with the staff, encouraged patients to become comfortable again with bodies that had been violated. Concentrating on the dance movements disrupts negative thoughts, and aids breathing and digestion. Aromatherapy hand-massage, a last-minute inclusion in the program, provided an opportunity for the women to accept and enjoy the touch of another person. The pain inflicted in rape torture makes all touch threatening to some women. From observing the role-play I realised that women who had bladder or bowel fistulas as a result of penetration during violent rape might be disgusted by the smell of their own bodies. Others said that women who had been raped couldn't forget the smell of the rapists. The counsellors readily agreed that the fragrant oils used in the massage might help with these issues and I managed to find enough bottles of perfumed hand lotion in the market for each participant to use with patients for as long as the supply lasted.

I didn't know if all the participants appreciated the value of these activities to the physical and emotional wellbeing of patients, but they did find them personally entertaining and relaxing. Reflecting on what I'd learnt about the lives of the staff at the hospital, I realised that given I had such a short time to work and couldn't communicate directly with the patients, helping the staff was probably the most useful contribution I could make.

In the course of my time here, these people had shared their own lives with me. None had escaped the violence. All had experienced several traumatic events – losing their homes or witnessing family members being killed or wounded. Some were themselves survivors of rape. One had lost every member of her family when the Rwandan army advanced on her village in 1996 and massacred the entire population. And yet one of their tasks was to go out to the often-insecure rural areas and bring survivors of the brutal assaults back to the hospital for treatment.

Figure 1.1: With some of the Heal Africa Hospital staff who participated in my trauma counselling workshop

*Figure 1.2: Staff participating in my workshops role-play counselling
a rape trauma survivor*

***

It's now more than three weeks since I arrived in Congo, and it's time to say goodbye to my inspiring new friends at the hospital. This morning I made the bone-jarring hour-long car trip from Maji to the centre of the city for the last time. In this final session with the staff who've come to the workshops, we've discussed the relevance of what was shared. I gave out the evaluation forms I'd prepared, and on the whole the participants' responses were courteous and complimentary. Nevertheless, I have mixed feelings about the past weeks. Nothing has turned out the way I planned.

I promise to keep in contact with everyone via emails to Zico, but life is so unpredictable in Congo that any of the people I've got to know could be dead tomorrow. I stumble over the Swahili farewell and blessing I've practised, but get applauded for the effort anyway. Now there are tearful goodbyes. The young literacy teacher, Kavira, crushes an envelope into my hand as she hugs me close. Impatient with all the emotion, Zico announces he will give me a tour of the hospital. I've already visited the transit ward to meet the eighty rape survivors waiting for fistula repair surgery and the overcrowded intensive care ward where fourteen of them had surgery on just one day. However, I've seen nothing of the rest of the hospital so I'm pleased by the prospect of a tour. While I wait for him to say his farewells, I open the envelope from Kavira and read the short note – in English! I had no idea she knew any Engish. I read, 'This is to thank you for coming to Congo and for all that you gave me.' And there is a US$5 note enclosed. I'm overwhelmed – people here often have to live on this amount for a week.

Still incredibly moved by this undeserved tribute, I follow Zico into a ward. People in this small, overcrowded room look really sick. There's no space between the dozen or so iron beds and the patients' belongings are stored beside them on the beds. I know the toilets are in a separate building some distance away and I wonder how patients manage to get there, because no staff are about and call buttons don't exist here.

A little girl, maybe eight or nine years old, sits up as we edge single-file up the aisle by her bed. Suddenly she's alert and excited, pointing at me and then at herself. I can't understand what she's saying. It could be in Swahili or one of several hundred languages spoken in this wide, geographically diverse country of many tribes. Zico is frowning at her and shaking his head. 'What is she saying?' I ask as she dives across the bed to the plastic bag containing her few possessions and pulls out some papers, waving them at me.

'She says her name is Barbara too, but it's unlikely. She is just reading your name tag. You mustn't trust these people,' Zico warns. But he takes the papers and scans them for her details. It is true, her name is Barbara. She reaches out both hands to me in a gesture I understand too well.

Zico laughs. 'She is asking you to take her home with you.'

One of the women, cradling her baby in a nearby bed, has been listening and joins in in French. 'She is an orphan. Her relatives brought her here very sick and abandoned her without leaving any contact details. So now she is better she has nowhere to go.'

'What was her illness,' I ask.

'Typhoid. This is the infectious diseases ward. We all have typhoid.'

Zico grabs my arm and hustles me out the door, ending this impromptu tour of the hospital. 'I didn't know,' he says.

I look back and through my tears see little Barbara, still sitting there, her arms outstretched towards me.

Figure 1.3: Rape trauma survivors waiting for surgery at HEAL Africa Hospital, 2009

Chapter 2

Meanwhile, be happy – August 2010

My body responds in perfect harmony with the beat of the drum and the movements of the people around me. There is something natural and compelling about this simple circular dance, deep in the heart of Africa. We dance in the unrelenting heat of an equatorial sun. We are all sweating copiously and I feel the black grit of the crushed lava from our impromptu dance floor settle on my face. The drum is an old upturned yellow jerry can. My ragged dance partners are arguably the world's most disadvantaged people: Pygmies, forced from their forest homes and barely tolerated in a new and hostile environment. But sheer joy is the shared emotion at this moment, as if we are the most blessed of all people. One friend explains, 'Surely we will know tears and sorrows soon enough. Meanwhile, be happy!'

**

When I returned to Australia from Congo in September last year I told my family I would 'never do that again'. Famous last words! It's 2010 and to my surprise, here I am in this remote and dangerous place at the end of three incredible weeks, reflecting on so many privileged experiences and promising to return as soon as I can organise the next visit.

Last year in my post-trip report to Lyn Lusi, who coordinated the allied health programs at HAH and who had issued the initial invitation for me to volunteer at the hospital, I confided that despite all my efforts to prepare and my previous international experience I had never anticipated the challenges Congo presented. I felt I really hadn't made a significant contribution to the hospital. Lyn understood perfectly, yet expressed her hope that I'd come again, and told me that the staff were already asking for me to return. Her entreaties and the opportunity to make a difference, even in a small way, overcame my reservations.

I left Australia this year confident that I knew what to expect of the journey. It was relatively predictable, although the flight from South Africa was so late getting into Kenya that I arrived breathless at the departure gates, the last passenger to board the flight into Rwanda, the only one that day. I made the flight, but the new luggage I'd bought to replace the bag that had been broken into on the last trip, didn't. Fortunately, Innocent, a long-lost Rwandan friend who I'd met when he was studying in Australia in 1995, was waiting for me at Kigali airport. After an emotional reunion, we registered the problem with the Kenya Airways representative, who assured me my bag would be there on the next flight at 3 a.m. tomorrow if I cared to wait around for it. I didn't, and instead took the opportunity to book into a hotel and spend the next couple of days in Rwanda.

I visited the Genocide Museum and the projects of Barakabaho, an agency helping genocide survivors which is administered by Innocent for the Anglican Church. The next day I followed Innocent along narrow, slippery mud paths, fearful of falling to my death, to visit his clients in their red clay huts on the terraced hillsides high above Kigali. The stories survivors told me are the stuff of nightmares. One young woman was nine years old when drug- and alcohol-crazed men invaded her home and hacked her parents to death. The disfiguring scars across her face, head, arms and breast are evidence of her terrified attempts to twist and turn away from the machete blows. She survived, but is scarred physically and psychologically for life.

After two memorable days in Kigali, Deo, my driver from 2009, came to the hotel to take me on to Goma, the capital of North Kivu province of the Democratic Republic of the Congo. As he bent to put my errant luggage in the boot of the car, I saw the back of his head and the frightful scars left by a machete attack that somehow he too had survived. On the long drive to Goma he told me his story and how all his younger sisters had been slaughtered in a convent school during those horrific three months in 1994. I suspect everyone I meet here has a story to tell, but in the interests of reconciliation people put aside the impulse for revenge and refuse to identify as members of the rival tribes; 'We are all Rwandans'.

The border crossing was just as chaotic as last year, and the process as drawn out and confusing, but I'd expected nothing less. This year I'd booked to stay downtown at a Christian guesthouse called the Bungwe that I'd been advised was a safe place for me to stay. It was just a short walk to the hospital so I was spared the drive from Maji every day along unsealed narrow alleys where drivers had to have nerves of steel to negotiate past other vehicles. Staying downtown meant I saw more of the city and the life of the people than had been possible last visit. Goma is really still a frontier shanty town. Most of the million residents live in single-storey cabins of timber or tin without running water, sanitation, power, postal services or garbage collection. The lava brick houses of the elite built on the shores of Lake Kivu, many of which are rented by international aid agencies, are the exception, having their own electricity generators and water-storage tanks. Their steep gabled roofs and ornate facades remind me of the pictures of houses in European children's stories like *Hansel and Gretel*.

The city is overshadowed by three active volcanoes. Nyiragongo, almost four kilometres high and one of the most active volcanoes in the world, is said to spew out more pollution in ash and noxious gases in one day than all the pollution in France in one year. At this time of year, the end of the dry season, you can't see the sky. The volcano is really only visible at night as a pulsing red glow high above the city. A film of dust covers everything, clogs my nose and throat, and irritates my eyes. When Nyiragongo erupted in 2002, a third of Goma was enveloped in a 40 kilometre-an- hour flow of molten lava hundreds of metres wide. Areas of the city still remind me of photos of a moonscape, yet some of the three hundred thousand displaced people are trying to build homes on the rough lava, erecting timber frames that sit at impossible angles on the uneven surface. Close to another million people, displaced by the ongoing conflict, are camping in or around the city, crowded into the two rooms of a relative's shack or in ragged makeshift shelters on vacant land. Just outside the city limits at Mugunga there is a sprawling long-term refugee camp for ten thousand people. Some were displaced in Congo and others were among the estimated one million who crossed the border from Rwanda after the genocide in 1994.

In the almost two years it had taken me to make contact with the Lusis at HAH and negotiate the bureaucracy to get into Goma, I had read whatever I could find on Congo. I learnt that long before the tragedy that has engulfed the country since the genocide in Rwanda, the Congolese people suffered under the Kings of Kongo who ruled a large area of present-day Congo from the fourteenth to the nineteenth centuries, and traded their people and the tribes they conquered as slaves throughout much of that time. This was followed by the brutality during the regime of King Leopold II of Belgium, and then the exploitation as a colony of Belgium. The Congolese haven't really enjoyed peace since Belgium granted independence in 1960, reluctantly and without due preparation. The geopolitics of the time allowed the rise of Mobutu, a ruthless dictator who came to power in 1965 and looted the country, which he renamed Zaire from 1971 until 1997. In the aftermath of the 1994 Rwandan genocide, those responsible for the violence fled across the border into Eastern Congo, an ever-present threat on their border that the Rwandan Government could not tolerate. The Rwandan military invaded and replaced Mobutu with their own ally, Laurent Kabila, father of the current president. The central government remained weak, a failed state unable to protect its borders and the rich natural resources of the land: diamonds, gold, copper, tin, cobalt, and the rare mineral coltan which is essential in the electronics industry. The eight nations surrounding Congo invaded in two opposing alliances in 1997 in what has been called 'The Great African War'. More than five million Congolese are thought to have died in that war.

Despite the peace treaty signed in 2002, people continue to die daily as more than thirty armed groups remain at war with each other and with the central government, terrorising the population of Eastern Congo. 'When elephants fight, the grass gets trampled,' people quote the old saying. Some militias aim to control the land and the rich natural resources, some are supported by outside forces with political goals, and others are formed to protect their communities and retaliate against rival groups. Even while I was there I heard that villages north of Goma in an area called Walikale had been ransacked and burnt to the ground and two hundred women raped.

***

At the Bungwe I'm woken at dawn every day by the call to prayer from a nearby mosque. It seems like a good way to begin my day, which is sure to hold many challenges. A couple of resident ghost-grey cats keep out the rats I am told overrun other hotels. I try to befriend them but they eye me warily and keep their distance. I am close to Kivu markets and can explore the town, although my friends are reluctant for me to go anywhere on my own. I asked for a map of the city so that I wouldn't get lost, only to find there are none. One evening not far from the guesthouse I met a little girl who sold me an avocado. She was afraid to go home until she had some cash to help feed the family. I meet and share stories with local and international guests. I have to try my schoolgirl French, although Vietnamese is my second language and all too often I think I'm speaking French when in fact I've switched into Vietnamese! The locals mix in a few words of Swahili with their French just to add to my confusion.

At the Bungwe restaurant I can invite new friends and colleagues to eat with me and teach me more about life here. On one wonderful weekend, I was included as a guest at a traditional Tutsi wedding held in the Bungwe's garden. New friends seated either side of me gave a running commentary on the proceedings. The multiple ceremonies began with the entrance of the bride's relatives dressed in their traditional warriors' outfits, long grass headdresses waving and spears shaking. They confronted the prospective bridegroom, who impatiently rejected the maidens presented to him until at last his chosen partner came forward. Then began the negotiations for the bride price with a delegation of the groom's male relatives wearing traditional long, toga-like robes and what looked a lot like boaters' hats. This was followed by a civil ceremony and finally a Christian blessing. The bride and her bevy of half a dozen maids and their partners changed their matching costumes in keeping with the nature of each ceremony. In a sign of the times and the HIV/AIDS threat, I learnt that when a couple register their marriage with the civil authorities they must provide evidence that they are not HIV positive.

Figure 2.1: Traditional marriage ceremony of Tutsi tribespeople at the Bungwe guesthouse in Goma

The first day back at HAH, I was overwhelmed by the warmth of the welcome and thankful that I'd taken the risk to return. So many volunteers promise continuing relationships, but once they leave Congo they are never heard from again. A team of Australian medical personnel who've been coming to the hospital and teaching in their various specialisations for several years are an exception. Consequently, as another Australian I benefited from the level of credibility they've established with the staff.

A total of forty-six people attended the three seminars this year. Last year I learnt that women and girls were not the only ones subjected to sexual violence so I called one seminar Protect the Little Children and offered it to staff working specifically with children in the hospital and also in some community programs. Mostly the content was about the stages of child development and the ways to identify children who had been sexually assaulted or subjected to physical assault or neglect. Because some of the participants didn't know each other very well I began with an exercise which encourages people to relax and engage with one another. They all took a photo from a random selection I had prepared and shared what it meant to them. One woman had chosen a photograph of a hippopotamus, remarking that it reminded her of her uncle. I laughed: 'He must be a big man?' 'No,' she shook her head sadly. 'He went to the river and a hippopotamus ate him!'

The second seminar for the psychosocial counsellors was Strategies for Healing Mind and Spirit, which introduced ways to help sexual assault survivors understand the emotional and psychological wounds resulting from their traumatic experience. Physical wounds and the associated symptoms are obvious to the patients and to the health professionals, but the symptoms of emotional trauma are confusing and often concealed by the patients, fearful of being thought 'crazy'. Last year I'd also learnt that there were local staff, members of the cultural and language communities of their patients, who had years of experience working in this field and were more skilled than I am. For them I offered a Train the Trainers workshop to prepare them to train new staff.

I was encouraged when people turned off their mobile phones, listened intently to the interpretation, asked questions and contributed eagerly in discussions. Sessions often went overtime, and when I would suggest a break, participants declared they had come to learn and not to drink tea. In all three workshops people shared cases which were often heartrending, and in the case of the assault on children quite sickening. Once again, I was struck by the many traumas in the lives of the staff members themselves. Additional pressure was obvious for some staff who were facing unemployment because the short-term European funding grants to the hospital had come to an end due to the Global Financial Crisis in Europe. The fragility of life came home to me forcefully when I asked about the literacy teacher Kavira who had given me the US$5 last year. They told me she had died of a *tombe malade* (severe illness), probably before it was even diagnosed.

***

The seminars are over, certificates presented at the chapel service, graduation celebrated. Today at last I've left the city to meet a group of Pygmies camped near a village called Mubambiro, located about 30 kilometres west of Goma not far from a market town called Sake. The active volcano looming over this area is the enormous Nyamulagira. I'm accompanied by an interpreter and Tuteene, the relative of a friend in Australia, who is my bridge to this group of Pygmies. Tuteene comes from the Batembo tribe and has travelled by ferry across the lake from his home in the adjoining province of South Kivu. The Batembo are descendants of the union of a Pygmy woman and a Bantu tribesman and share some of the stigma suffered by the Pygmies. Pygmies are on the very bottom of the hierarchy of tribes, sometimes not even considered to be *Bantu* (people). Every time I meet Tuteene he's wearing a different outfit; so far I've seen five outfits in five vibrant colours: red, blue, green, mustard yellow and brown, worn with matching waistcoat and hat. I suspect this studied elegance might be a strategy to improve his social status. Today he is wearing the brilliant crimson ensemble.

The roads getting out of Goma city are in such disrepair and are so congested it takes over an hour to get to Mubambiro. I was told that only 10 per cent of roads in all of Congo are sealed. In some sections the potholes are bigger than the islands of eroded bitumen on this main highway. I pity the men, some just boys, who are riding pushbikes loaded down with three or four 50-kilogram bags of charcoal. Or those pushing similar loads on the unique-to-Congo half-scooter, half-wheelbarrow *chukudus*. As the driver swerves around the giant puddles and oncoming vehicles I bounce about in the back of the vehicle as if riding a mechanical bull. The Congolese with me tell me, 'If you ask us which side of the road we drive on in Congo we have to say, "It depends. If there is a hole on the right side of the road we drive on the left. If there is a hole on the left then we drive on the right."

Once we leave the city limits behind I delight in the views of spectacular mountains rising above an expanse of almost impenetrable bushland, all that is left of the forest in this part of Virunga National Park, and the shimmering waters of Lake Kivu. The drive isn't uneventful. We are stopped by armed and suspicious military at several checkpoints and at one of these there is hot debate about whether or not we can continue the journey. I've heard that two Americans were stopped recently in that area. In trying to retrieve his passport one of them was accused of inadvertently causing one of the officers to fall and break his leg. The Americans spent several nights in a Congolese prison before their diplomats were able to get them released. I don't know who might come to my rescue if I get into trouble since Australia has no diplomats in Congo. Smiles and a US$5 gift solve the immediate problem and we pass on.

The Pygmies I've come to meet are sharing an unofficial camp with other displaced people from the various tribes in this area. I've been told that 96 per cent of the general population here have been displaced over the past fifteen years. Some have tried repeatedly to return to their subsistence farms in the fertile valleys of Masisi, only to lose everything again as the conflict ebbs back and forth. The Pygmies are forced to live at the back of this camp at Mubambiro where they are the last to know when there is a rare distribution of aid. They usually miss out altogether.

Around two hundred Pygmies are here, most of them members of two extended family groups. They tell me they come from the forests on Mount Shove, close by Nyiragongo Volcano. It is fifteen years now since the presence of rebel strongholds in the forest and government policy forced them from the forest verge and even longer since they left their traditional home in the deep forest. I was told that after their exile these people had been granted no special status as custodians of the forest resources. Pygmies in other provinces could continue to enter the forest to harvest fruits and nuts and wild honey, but the people from the Virunga Forest so close to the Rwandan border returned to the forest at their peril. Consequently, since their expulsion they've been forced to live as nomads and beggars, displaced time and again by Congolese and Rwandan militias, bandits and mining companies. At one time they were offered land of their own at Nyabirere not too far from Mubambiro. They soon discovered it was unsafe and every time they began to establish a village for themselves rebel bands attacked and left them destitute and on the move once more.

Estimates vary but perhaps as many as three hundred thousand Pygmies are surviving across Central Africa. They are probably the first peoples of this area. The anthropologist Colin Turnbull lived with a band of Pygmies in the forests of North Kivu in 1957–58. The only source of information I had on Pygmies and their traditional way of life came from his account *The Forest People*, first published in 1961. He reported that archaeologists had found evidence that twenty thousand to thirty thousand years ago, for some reason, their ancestors must have taken refuge in the dense forests of the region. Over this period, with limited exposure to sunlight and subjected to the hazards and illnesses prevalent in the environment, they have acquired an inherited genetic mutation that makes them resistant to the human growth hormone. They are fully mature around twelve years of age and are usually 122–152 centimetres tall.

In English, the word 'pygmy' has taken on a pejorative connotation as not just small, but inadequate. In the sparse literature about Pygmies, I read that the word is derived from the Greek word for the length of a normal human forearm. I wondered if perhaps, having heard about them but never having actually seen a Pygmy, the Greeks imagined them to be tiny mythical beings, like hobbits. When I talk about Pygmies in Australia, some people object because of the negative associations and suggest I should use the Swahili words, *Mbuti* (singular) *Bambuti* (plural) which are used for Pygmies in this area. But again, I read in the literature that the word for the forest-dwellers in the various tribal languages (e.g. *Baka, Batwa*) is always pejorative and distinguishes them from *Bantu* (people), so I continue to use the English word 'Pygmy'.

Here in Mubambiro, some people have intermarried with local tribes and it seems to me that the children of these unions do not carry the gene as they are already taller than their Pygmy parent and easily pass as Bantu unless they declare their heritage. Or perhaps life in the open sunshine and outside the hazards of the forests is already affecting the physical development of this generation.

I am no stranger to the miserable conditions in refugee camps across the world. Nevertheless, the plight of people here in this unofficial settlement is affecting me deeply. The shelters are mostly flimsy grass huts the size of one-man tents. The grass is dry, already disintegrating, and soon tropical storms will sweep through the camp and surely wash the huts away. In the Bantu area of the camp people are ashamed of their poor circumstances and pointedly warn me not to take photos. But Alexis, who appears to be in charge of the Pygmy area, leads me on a tour here emphasising the absolute destitution everyone is enduring. He introduces Nyota (Star), a sixteen-year-old girl with a new baby, and she shows me her entire possessions: a tin dish for food, water and washing, and a rug for the cold nights.

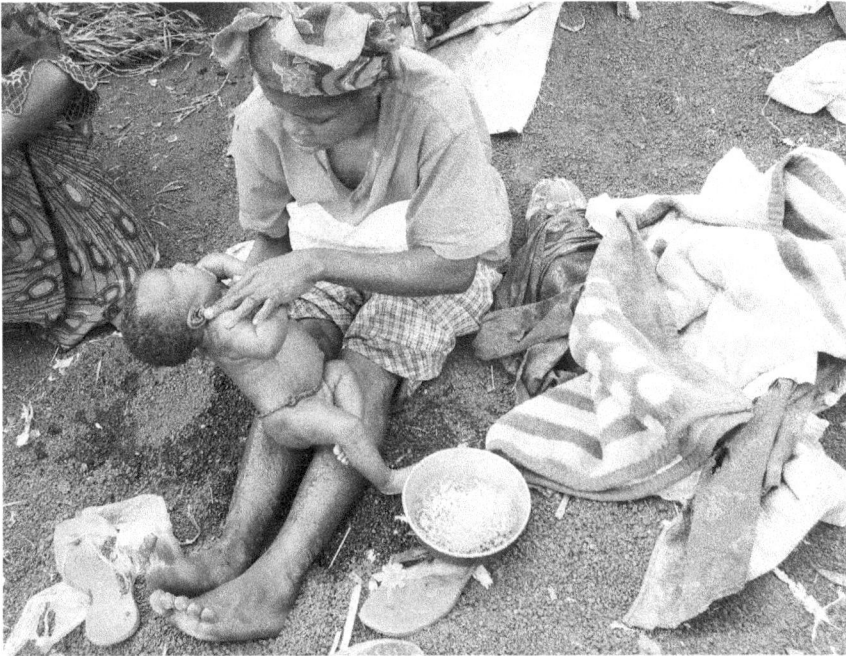

Figure 2.2: Sixteen-year-old Nyota with her baby son and her entire possessions

Although we are so close to the Equator we are 2000 metres above sea level, and on the shores of the lake the temperature drops down to nine or ten degrees Celsius at night. People live hand to mouth. Most families keep hunger at bay by cooking a weak cabbage or cassava leaf soup on open charcoal fires, with maybe a handful of rice or beans thrown in if they are lucky that week. I know that even many staff employed at the hospital eat only once a day. These Pygmy families eat this frugal meal maybe every two days.

The children, who make up more than half the population of the camp, are filthy and dressed in an assortment of rags and threadbare adult-sized

T-shirts. But they laugh and chatter as they follow me around. Some clutch a well-chewed piece of sugarcane; Tuteene tells me it staves off hunger. Almost all show signs of malnutrition: runny noses, hacking coughs, opens sores, skeletal limbs and huge umbilical hernias on swollen bellies. Not surprisingly, little girls, and some little boys have a younger sibling on their hip for whom they are the day-long carer. One group has a ball they've made out of disintegrating scraps of plastic bags twisted together. Another child has an improvised hoop made from the rim of a bicycle wheel and expertly demonstrates his skill in keeping it bowling along the uneven ground with a short stick.

[Figure 2.3: Some of the Pygmy children on the day we met]

Figure 2.4: The proud hoop-bowler with friends

Figure 2.5: Vumilia's only shelter

Vumilia, who barely comes up to my shoulder (and I only stand at 156 centimetres), was introduced to me as the leader of the women. Like most of the women she looks to be pregnant and the several layers of cloth she has wound around her body are the only clothes she possesses. At the end of a tour of the camp she leads me through the haphazard collection of huts to the furthest corner. 'She says this is a very dangerous place for women,' my interpreter tells me. 'Both rebel and government soldiers, far from home and looking for sex, will rape a woman if she comes here alone at night.' Vumilia is pointing at a huge pit, partially screened off from view by sheets of tattered canvas attached to bamboo poles. It is the communal toilet for the hundreds of people camped here. Quite apart from the danger of encountering rapists, I wonder how a heavily pregnant woman could maintain her balance on the boards across the deep, smelly pit.

I couldn't bear to leave without at the very least offering some sort of assistance, and gave Vumilia and Alexis a solemn promise to help, adding that I didn't know how I could best help them. They said they would call a meeting with everyone to tell me what would be of the most assistance. While the meeting was being organised, I decided to go to nearby Sake market to buy what would be some evidence of my commitment to them. The interpreter helped me buy a 50-kilogram bag of rice and another of beans and enough biscuits for each of the children to have a small packet for themselves. Returning to the camp we gave a lift to a Pygmy woman who was carrying a plastic bag containing what looked like dirty water. She explained that she'd begged a fisherman in the market to give her the water he'd used to wash the knife with which he'd gutted his catch. She would cook her cabbage leaves in it to give the soup some fishy flavour.

By the time we got back to Mubambiro the people were gathered in a central place in the camp, some perched on lava rocks. A murmur of anticipation rose as we came to the front. The leading men stepped forward to tell me the decision they'd reached. 'The Forest was our Father, the Forest gave us food and clothes, homes and medicines. Now we have nothing and must beg for our food. We don't want our children to have to be beggars like us, so we need you to pay the fees for them to go to school so they will be educated.'

Figure 2.6: The community meet to tell me their decision

I understood their reasoning, marvelled at their insight and the wisdom of the decision, but wondered how I could possibly meet the expectations I had raised. I'd had in mind something like replacing the canvas around the pit-toilet. Roughly estimating the number of children of primary school age, I guessed the request would mean school fees for at least fifty children but had no idea how much my rash promise was going to cost me. After all my experience working in and teaching about international work, I wondered how I'd been so naive. If only I'd stayed to observe the meeting I would've been able to step in and set some boundaries. Too late for regrets!

While I consulted with Tuteene about a way to resolve the embarrassing situation I found myself in, the children were assembled for the distribution of the biscuits, and the headmen took control of the division of the rice and beans for every family. Tuteene runs his own relief agency for Pygmies and Batembo in South Kivu and today proved his worth as a negotiator and adviser. He went to the nearby primary school to find out exactly what the fees might be for each child. When he returned, he reported that the principal was initially unwilling to enrol Pygmy children, but his attitude softened when he heard a 'rich' foreigner might be involved. However, he had conditions: the children were to have uniforms, sandals, bags and books; they were to be clean and have their heads shaved. Moreover, the annual fees must be paid in full up front.

We leant against a convenient lava boulder and added up what all this would cost. The fees for the estimated fifty children amounted to US$3000 and Tuteene thought he could organise the uniforms, sandals, books and bags, and soap and razors to shave heads, for another US$3000. My bank balance had been depleted by the two trips to Congo so far but I'd been saving up to replace my twenty-year-old car. I recalled that the mechanic who had looked after this car ever since I bought it had told me that if ever I wanted to sell it he wanted it, as it was still in such good condition. I decided I didn't need a new car and we were able to announce that after I returned to Australia I would send the funds for the children to go to school.

A new car could never have brought me the satisfaction I felt as people realised that I was promising to meet their request. With that and the prospect of rice and beans for dinner, everyone, regardless of age or disability, is dancing with me.

Figure 2.7: Some of the children selected for study at the local school

Figure 2.8: Dancing to the jerry-can drum

Chapter 3

Land matters – February 2011

I am stunned. I ask the interpreter to confirm what the school principal has just said. It's true: one of the Pygmy boys, Dieudonne, has come second in his class after just six months in school. For a fatherless child from such a deprived and disrupted background to have achieved so much is amazing.

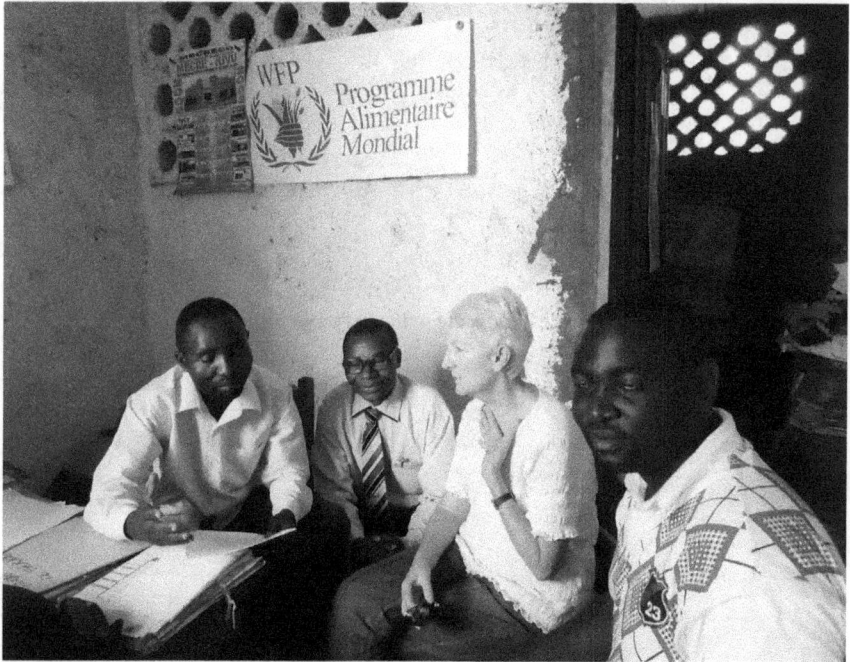

Figure 3.1: I am amazed to learn that Dieudonne has come second in his class after only six months in school

This is the first opportunity I've had to come out to Mubambiro since I arrived back in Congo for the third visit. Looking around at the disorganised office and conscious of the bedlam from nearby classrooms, I suspect the standard of education here is very low. Seven hundred children are enrolled in this primary school, one hundred children in every class, at least four to a desk. Although education isn't free in Congo there aren't enough places for those who can pay. Too many schools, like other public buildings, have been destroyed or abandoned in the conflict. The remaining buildings must operate morning and afternoon sessions and children only go to school for half a day. Even so, no more than 25 per cent of school-age children do so. There is added incentive for parents to send their children to this school: World Food Program funds a daily meal of cassava and plantain porridge for the children in this area of high displacement and disadvantage. The cooking pots and utensils are all piled up at the back of the classrooms.

Figure 3.2: Pygmy children in class at the local primary school. Note at the back of the room the pots and pans for preparing the World Food Program daily meal

I'm anxious to know if all fifty-five of the Pygmy children we enrolled after I visited last September are regularly attending school. The principal assures me attendance is good. I ask if the other children accept the presence of the Pygmy children because I was warned last year about the widespread perception that Pygmies are less intelligent than other people. He nods his head vigorously. Not only the children of the local Bantu tribes but the parents too have changed their opinion of the Pygmies. 'They see them come to school clean and wearing new uniforms,' he says. Then he smiles knowingly. 'And you see, because you paid fees for the year in full, we have been able to provide new materials for all the children. So, of course they are happy!'

***

When I returned to Australia after the first encounter with the Pygmies at Mubambiro last year I couldn't wait to tell my friends about them. The interest to help with their education snowballed. When Tuteene requested funds for some of the older children to go to high school I had no trouble finding sponsors. After I'd made it clear I could only sponsor children at primary school last year I'd been haunted by the disappointment on the faces of two teenage boys, Eric and Heritier, and two young men, Munguiko and Kayese, who'd hoped I would sponsor them to continue the studies they'd been able to pursue for a few years previously. It was wonderful that my friends wanted to pay fees for them too, and thus educate future leaders for the community.

Even while I was getting together all the documents for my current visit, Tuteene contacted me with another problem confronting the Pygmies. Their flimsy shelters made out of sticks and reeds gathered on the lake shores provided no protection from the driving rain of the wet season now upon them. School uniforms, books and bags were saturated and many of the children, already in poor health due to malnutrition and parasites, were quite sick after spending days in wet clothes. I sent funds for them to buy canvas sheeting to cover the huts but knew it was a poor, short-term solution.

Optimistic about the interest to help from Australian friends, I emailed Tuteene and asked if I could provide materials so people could build more permanent structures. He explained that this was a bad idea. The wealthy man who owned the land where people were camping would immediately want to charge rent for the use of his land. It was unlikely that many of the Pygmies, if any, could pay him. Pygmies have no rights, no legal protection, so he would evict them, take over their homes and find other displaced people who could pay. What they needed first was land of their own.

This was uppermost in my mind just hours before I left Sydney, when I learnt that the policy at the Congolese border with Rwanda had changed and visitors could no longer purchase a visa there. Although I didn't know if it was possible, I decided to fly out of Australia as scheduled and apply for my visa at the new Congolese Embassy in Kigali once I arrived in Rwanda. At first it looked like the process would take weeks but eventually I persuaded the Embassy staff to let me meet the Ambassador even though I hadn't made an appointment in advance. I was ushered into his office by his nervous secretary and stood in silence for fully five minutes before he looked up and acknowledged my presence. I apologised for my intrusion and presented him with an Australian calendar. Then he revealed that he had enjoyed a visit to Australia some years ago which was why he was giving me 'special consideration'. Still, I'd lost precious days waiting to get into Congo and had less time for all the activities I'd planned there. Moreover, the Embassy staff forgot to add one of the required stamps to my passport. Consequently, when I arrived at the Congolese border I had to pay an additional $100 to get into the country.

I was anxious to get on with the HAH workshop, which was with the small group of psychosocial counsellors I was hoping would become trainers for new staff. While I respected their experience and cultural knowledge, I thought that they needed a clear model to guide their own practice and to pass on to other staff. The Brief Intervention for Trauma Survivors (BITS), a model which had been devised by Brisbane-based psychiatrist Steven Stathis, seemed most appropriate. In psychoeducation, which is the first step in intervention according to this model, the symptoms commonly experienced as a consequence of trauma are described so that survivors come to understand that their own physical and psychological reactions are normal. In the second step survivors are given the opportunity to tell their story, but rather than dwelling on the details, they are encouraged, once the nature of their ordeal has been expressed, to focus on the symptoms that bother them in the present. While trauma survivors need to know that their stories are heard and believed, research supports the idea that repeated accounts of the trauma can plunge them back into the state of terror and helplessness that they were in at the time of the event and also entrenches memories that might otherwise gradually become less disturbing. Talking about the after-effects of their ordeal shifts attention from the past to the present and their current needs, and then to potential ways to meet those needs. This step connects with the third step in the model where survivors identify strategies to keep themselves and others safe. In this regard, I now knew HAH staff had initiated Women Stand Up Together empowerment and training programs in the rural areas for women who had been at the hospital. The final step in the model is for the survivors to resist taking the blame for the assault and to place the blame entirely on the perpetrator.

After the workshops, I met Lyn Lusi and discussed my intention to buy land for the Pygmies. She warned me that ownership of land is at the heart of many problems in Congo. Traditionally, land had been in the gift of tribal chiefs, but in modern times the state had taken over regulation of land ownership. When the conflict began in the mid-1990s, people fled the lands their families and tribe had farmed for generations. When the fighting temporarily subsided, people who took the risk of going into an insecure area settled on the available land, and the former owners had no recourse even if they returned and tried to reclaim it. This process still happens again and again as conflict erupts back and forth across the region, and no one can say who really owns the land. Disputes rage on and are further complicated when international companies come in to mine the rich resources of traditional farmland and forested areas and hire their own militia to protect their investment.

Undaunted, I was still hoping there would be a way to cut through all these barriers and establish a village of their own for the people who had won my heart. Some people who identified as Pygmies had actually cleared a space and made villages in the forest, but most of the people I was working with came from the deep forest. They told me that before they were forced out of the forest they did not own land, did not settle in villages, did not build any sort of shelter and did not farm land. They lived in small family groups, sheltering under rocks or overhanging branches, hunting and gathering in a particular area and moving on when the resources there were depleted. Once an extended family reached around thirty people, some would break away and form their own group in another area, usually with a minimum of conflict. Now displaced from the forest and living in Mubambiro, several extended families had combined for safety in a way they wouldn't have done normally.

Despite her misgivings about my plan, Lyn introduced me to Maitre Martin, a lawyer on a retainer from HEAL Africa Hospital, and I asked him to help me with the process of buying land for the Pygmy families at Mubambiro. A young Australian–Congolese man related to Tuteene accompanied us to interpret for me. Just before we ventured out to Mubambiro for the first time this visit, Lyn remembered that HAH had purchased land for a group of people who sounded very much like the group I was helping. She found the receipt of purchase for the land and asked me to check up on these people and their situation.

Maitre Martin advised that as a matter of courtesy we must meet with the traditional high chief of the area to keep him informed of our purposes, even though in fact his powers were now limited by the state. We met in Goma in the grounds of the university and presented him with a bottle of wine as tribute. It turned out that he did us no favours by alerting the local chief at Mubambiro that a foreigner was on her way intent on buying land for Pygmies in his area.

Figure 3.3: From left: Tuteene, me, the traditional High Chief and our Attorney Martin

When we arrived at Mubambiro, ten of the leading Pygmy men were gathered together prepared to accompany Martin, the interpreter and myself to inspect some available plots. The local chief, having been forewarned, had also arrived on the scene and told me he had ideal land to show me which he would be happy to sell. He led us way off the road up hilly, rough terrain for at least thirty minutes. I followed blindly, often stumbling and at one stage fell into a ditch and had to be hoisted out. He kept telling me it was 'just a little further on'. It wasn't until I was balancing precariously on a narrow tree trunk across a swollen stream that I called a halt and told him I wasn't interested in going any further. I turned to the delegation of Pygmies and asked their opinion.

Even before I heard the translation I knew they weren't happy about what the chief had to say about this. For a few moments, it looked like the situation would escalate into physical violence with the infuriated Pygmy men shouting defiance at this traditional authority figure. The interpreter reported, 'I can't believe what just happened. Pygmies never disobey a Bantu chief. But when this man told them they must tell you to buy his land, they refused! They told him that you have promised to listen to them and they don't have to obey him now.'

The old chief must have been dismayed and I was persuaded to give him US$5 for his trouble, which he accepted with bad grace and disappeared. We traipsed around for the best part of a day to find a more suitable site. I was soaked to the skin at one point when the skies opened with driving rain, thunder and lightning, and no shelter in sight. At last we decided on a flat and barren piece of land that happened to be adjacent to the piece of land purchased five years ago for the Pygmies by HAH. However, the owner of that land, who had been trusted by the Lusis, had taken the money but then forbidden the Pygmies to settle on it. Martin explained that what Lyn had given me was basically only a bill of sale. Until the land had been officially surveyed and registered in the name of the Pygmies at the Regional Lands Office, the former owner could maintain control. The Pygmies dared not defy him. That land had tripled in value since 2006 and I imagined he was hoping the people would move on from Mubambiro looking for a better situation and he could sell it again.

What followed in the next few days was a lesson on how to get things done in a society where family and tribal obligations are paramount. When we arrived at the Regional Lands Office, a quick word from Maitre Martin to the clerk at the front desk and we were ushered past a long line of people with petitions in hand and into the office of the head of department. The two men greeted each other traditionally, forehead to forehead, and the interpreter whispered to me that they were tribal brothers. Our mission was fast-tracked and very soon we were joined by two massive surveyors who accompanied us back to Mubambiro and proceeded to measure up the lands we were securing for the Pygmies. We ended up with four pieces that lie on either side of an unsealed road and give the Pygmies a little more than 2.5 acres of land for a village.

That evening back at the Bungwe, I was celebrating the day's outcome over a meal with Pastor Samuel. He had brought along a tribal brother, a very entrepreneurial man called Fabien. And he introduced a man called

Fred, who was working with the Seventh Day Adventist Rural Development Agency (ADRA), which had funds from the Danish Government to provide materials to build houses for vulnerable people in the area of Mubambiro. Instantly alerted to the possibility of enlisting Fred's aid for the Pygmies, I arranged to meet him the next day at his office outside Sake, the nearest town to Mubambiro, to discuss this and to view houses and other building projects he was managing for ADRA.

On my way to Sake the next day with an interpreter and a hired car and driver, I had a phone call from Maitre Martin. Some papers hadn't been lodged at the Regional Lands Office the previous day and they had to be presented urgently. The interpreter left me with the driver while he took a motorcycle ride back to Goma to attend to this. When we arrived at Fred's office, I transferred into his sturdy truck and we headed up the mountain on a narrow, winding unsealed road. We were some distance beyond Sake and still far from the main project he wanted me to see when our way was completely blocked by a broken-down vehicle. Fred decided it would be hours before that truck could be moved and we would have to walk on up the mountain to our goal at a place called Malehe.

Figure 3.4: On the narrow road to Malehe

I knew that bandits often blocked a road with some sort of accident and then ambushed travellers who tried to pass by on foot, but Fred set off confidently so I followed him up the steep mountainside for about twenty minutes to a plateau where the project was under construction. We were more than 2000 metres above sea level and I was struggling to breathe after the climb – and the panoramic view of the rolling green hills of this remote region gained from our lofty position was enough to take my breath away again. For the first time on my travels out of Goma, I saw wild African daisies, surprising splashes of bright pink among the hillside's lush vegetation. After inspecting the impressive projects he was managing, including a birthing clinic for women in the district, we walked back down the mountain to Fred's vehicle, where the truck was still blocking the rarely used road. On the walk we agreed that Fred would take on the organisation of housing the Pygmies on the land I'd secured. He would take a census of the legitimate residents, estimate the number of houses required and provide the building materials, set out the village, and hire an engineer/ architect to supervise the building. I would need to pay this man, Joseph, for his work and provide some small stipend for Fred's workmen to help the Pygmies actually build the houses.

Once back in his vehicle, Fred was in a hurry and we hurtled down the mountain, at every hairpin turn in danger of launching off the road and over the side. He asked if I was afraid but I pretended nonchalance. I left Fred at his office near Sake and continued down the mountain at a more sedate pace in the vehicle that was to take me back to Goma. After such a productive and active day I was tired but relaxed and must have been nodding off to sleep when we came to a sudden stop. A police vehicle barred our way and two armed men approached. I wasn't concerned until I realised the driver's black face had actually gone red. His hands were shaking as he fumbled around with some papers from the glove box, while obviously indicating to me to offer a bribe. From some notes in my pocket I peeled off a US one-dollar bill, and kept peeling until I had handed over sixteen. But still the police weren't happy. It was only then that I grasped the fact that the driver didn't have a valid driver's licence. And remembered that my phone was useless because there had been the usual power cut last night and I hadn't charged the battery.

One of the policemen got in the vehicle and the other came around to my side and opened the door. I was refusing to get out and sending up a silent prayer when I heard, in English, 'Barbara, what is wrong?' A vehicle had pulled up alongside us and there was Fabien, the man I'd met at the guesthouse only last night. I had no idea then and still don't know what he was doing in that area at that time: another angel to my rescue! He got between me and the policeman, smiling and laughing, and after a conversation I couldn't understand suddenly everyone was laughing and we were free to go.

Although I was quite shaken by this narrow escape, I wanted to make a quick stop at Mubambiro School to see the children in the afternoon classes before returning to Goma. I had colourful Australian calendars for each classroom. One with photos of our unique Australian birds caused a commotion, with the younger children squealing and peeping through their fingers in terror. They don't see wildlife here. The monkeys and all other animals and birds which once inhabited this area in abundance have been wiped out to provide food for starving people.

I was used to being mobbed by the children in Congo. Once they lost their fear of a white face they were fascinated as much by my white hair as by my white skin. But at the school, one little girl was increasingly desperate in trying to get my attention. She kept hopping after me grabbing my arm and pointing to her right foot, which was shoeless. I nodded, yes. I knew shoes got lost. Tuteene, in a sombre black outfit today, had joined us and I asked him to assure her we would replace her sandals. But he said it wasn't that the shoe was lost; her foot, when I looked more closely, was swollen from toes to ankle. On the underside of the foot there was a huge suppurating sore. Once I saw how serious her situation was, I wanted to meet her family and organise to take her back to HAH with me. However, it was already close to 5 p.m. and Tuteene and the driver were adamant that we must leave the area that minute. I knew from the visit last year that HAH local staff visiting community projects were strictly instructed to be on the road back to Goma by 5 p.m. or stay where they were. It would be equally dangerous for me as a foreigner to be on the road as to try to stay where I was. I opted for the road back to Goma. I promised I would be back the next day and we would get this child some treatment. In the car, Tuteene told me her name was Giselle, she was nine years old, an orphan who shared a small humpy with her older sister, the sister's husband and their three children.

Back at the Bungwe I was disappointed to find there was no power and so no water, much less hot water, to wash off the sweat and dust of the day. But the receptionist came knocking at my door with a bucket of water he had saved for me and heated on a charcoal stove! Even my physical exhaustion and his kindness above and beyond the call of duty couldn't stop me lying awake half the night thinking about Giselle.

Next day, travelling in a new car with a licensed driver, I spent the first few hours in the camp meeting with Joseph, the architect, to discuss his fee and the layout of the village of sixty-five houses. I also organised for the children to have a second set of uniforms, and I paid for sewing lessons for five of the Pygmy women and for three hand-operated sewing machines and other materials as required by the training program they were to join in Sake. I hoped they would eventually be able to make the uniforms for the village children. Friends in Sydney had wondered why Pygmy mothers didn't keep the children in clean and mended clothes. It is so hard to communicate the extent of the destitution of these people, who have to beg for a mouthful of food so can't even think about buying washing soap or needles and thread. One day in the camp I asked why the children had all lost the buttons on their shirts. The answer was that the buttons had been taken off and sold in the market to provide a meal or essential medicine for the family.

It was already mid-afternoon when I went to find Giselle. She was waiting for me, sitting on the stony ground outside her sister's humpy, her legs straight out in front of her. In the blazing hot sun she was grey-faced and shivering, a picture of misery. Obviously, she had developed a high temperature. The camp was full of soldiers patrolling that day because overnight two soldiers had been ambushed and killed in the area. I had made the right decision not to stay that night in the village! As I approached Giselle from one direction a soldier was approaching her from the other. Nearing the child, he raised his boot and I could see he meant to kick her out of his path. I charged him, yelling *Hapana!* (No!). I don't know who was more surprised, the soldier or myself, suddenly aware that I was threatening an armed man. He stopped in his tracks and the interpreter raced in to my defence. Fortunately, he knew some Lingala, the language spoken by the soldiers assigned in this area, who come from tribes in the western provinces of the country. He managed to explain who I was and that the Pygmy child was in my care. I wanted to relieve some of Giselle's symptoms and pulled out some paracetamol tablets I always carried for my own use, but Giselle's sister indicated she had no water to hand, let alone a cup for the child to take the tablets.

As we drove back to Goma with Giselle, the interpreter said the soldier had told him that life in the army was miserable, living off the land in conditions worse than the displaced families while corrupt generals withheld the pay of the lower ranks. In response to the troops' complaints that they hadn't been paid, a former president had infamously responded, 'You have guns, you don't need a salary.' Apparently, some commanders today still embraced that policy. And this disgruntled combatant said, 'We had to leave our homes and families to fight for these people, but no one here likes us.'

I'd also taken Giselle's sister, Shu Krani, and her three little children back to Goma with us. Initially the children had been wide-eyed with fear on their first ever ride in a vehicle, but when they'd realised the other children in the camp were running along beside the car cheering them, they'd sat up to wave back like celebrities. When we got to the hospital, the doctors in the tiny, cluttered emergency room had a hard time even examining Giselle's foot as she screamed at the top of her lungs and clung to me with all her might. After an X-ray and blood tests she was admitted to a ward, but the other patients tormented her mercilessly, confirming all I had heard about the relentless discrimination Pygmies were subjected to. In the end, I paid for a private room for her and the family. While they were there I arranged for the whole family to be assessed for health problems. When the results came in some days later, the four-year-old girl was half the weight for her age; the boy, not yet three years old, had tuberculosis; and all of them, including Shu Krani and the baby, had malaria and parasites.

At first it seemed Giselle might lose the foot: a huge abscess had formed over a plantar wart. But once the abscess had been lanced and kept clean and Giselle had had several courses of powerful antibiotics, it began to heal. It would leave a significant scar, but given Giselle's fragile health, if the abscess had been left untreated, she might have lost her life.

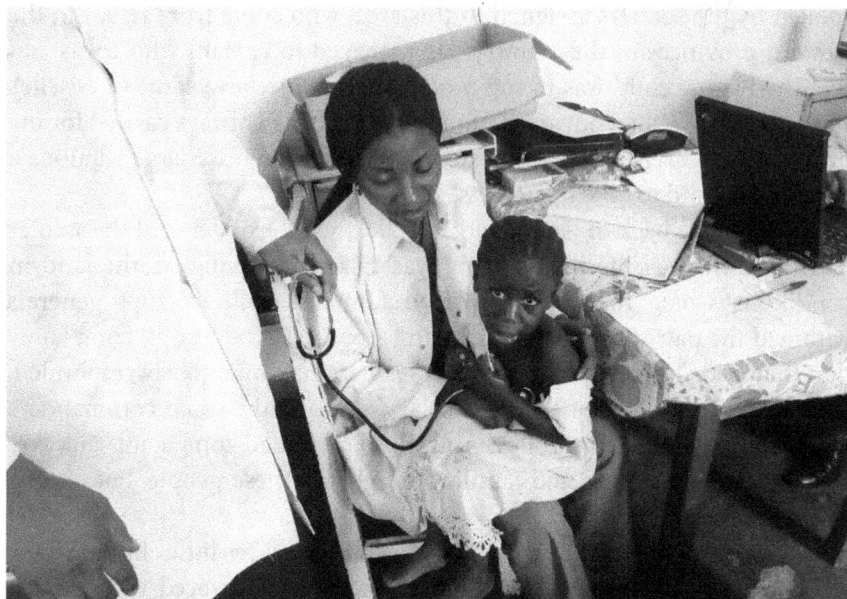

Figure 3.5: Giselle at Heal Africa Hospital with the orthopaedics nurse

There was time for one last trip out to Mubambiro. I made hasty visits to the senior high schools where Munguiko and Kayese, the two oldest Pygmy youths I was sponsoring, were preparing to sit the State Finals Examinations, equivalent to a Higher School Certificate and the door to university study. The principal told me that Munguiko was most likely to pass, being an excellent student. Back at the primary school, Jervais, the principal, had invited me to his office where I was introduced to Anselm, the principal of the Mubambiro junior high school. To this point, only two years of high school had been available beyond primary school, including for our boys, Eric and Heritier. I had contributed to the construction of another classroom for a third year of school so these older children would be able to continue their studies. Anselm was effusively grateful.

As always, I was frustrated by my inability to follow the rest of the conversation in a mixture of French and Swahili. I contained my impatience until finally the interpreter explained. While Dieudonne was doing so well and all of the Pygmy children would be able to continue in the school, they were at a disadvantage because their parents were not only illiterate in French, Swahili and their own language, but also had no understanding of the essential requirements of a formal education system. In spite of Jervais's earlier assurances, not all of the sponsored children were attending classes regularly. Many of them arrived late, unkempt, in dirty uniforms, and walked out of class if a parent came by to call them away. The Pygmy girls in particular were not making the most of the opportunity because too often they were expected to bring younger siblings to school, which of course was not permitted. However, Anselm had a scheme to set up a program to prepare the youngest children for school. He had found a small building in a nearby Bantu village which we could rent, and he had six women, trained teachers, who were willing to work with the children for a few dollars. All they needed now was my financial support.

I know all foreigners are fabulously rich in the minds of these people. And in fact I am wealthy in comparison to the majority of people I meet in this country of 80 per cent unemployment. Anselm pressed his point, urging me outside where he had organised the six teachers to assemble a horde of little children, grinning from ear to ear, applauding and yelling *Asante Mama Barabara* (Thanks, Mama Highway). My name, Barbara, is easily confused with the Swahili word for highway. I used to be greeted with calls of *mzungu mzee* (old foreigner), but I think Mama Highway might be a step up.

Figure 3.6: I couldn't resist the children's eagerness for a preschool

53

That evening back at the guesthouse I recalled that Chris Albany, rector of the church I attend in Sydney, had volunteered personal funds for any worthwhile project that might come up. I called Chris, oblivious to the time difference, and probably woke him and his wife. I described the need and the proposal for a preschool for the youngest children. Not only would they be prepared for school activities; we could give them a meal, provide some simple medicines and keep them safe while their older siblings were in school. Chris didn't hesitate to offer financial support for this project. His wife, Pam, had just been diagnosed with motor neurone disease – we would call the project 'Pamela's Preschool' in her honour.

Chapter 4

Building and business – September 2011

My heart always lifts as we leave the ugly outskirts of Goma city and see the mountains beyond rising up before us. Off to the right is Nyiragongo Volcano, half shrouded in clouds, and off to the left, past the dense, low-lying savannah shrubbery of that part of Virunga National Park, are the deep waters of Lake Kivu. They are all deadly dangerous, I know. The volcano is due for another major eruption and unpredictable surges of odourless methane gas emanating from the lake and the savannah floor have caused unsuspecting people to pass out and drown, or disappear in the impenetrable depths of the undergrowth.

I'm bouncing up and down with the motion of the car – the road is no better than on previous trips, if not worse. Suddenly I see something new in the distance: a patchwork of rectangular shapes glinting in the sun among the dark patches of a few struggling eucalyptus trees. It must be the iron roofs of the sixty-five houses in the new Pygmy village! 'Stop the car and let me take photos!' I say. Samuel agrees but urges me to be quick. There is a Congolese military camp in the same direction and a United Nations base. It is illegal to take photos of public buildings and military installations – photos that might be of use to rebels.

Figure 4.1: View of the new village from the road

55

This is my fourth visit to Congo and my first opportunity to see the village. I'm conscious of so many things to do in a short time because I've realised I can't stay more than two weeks this trip. Every visit I pick up parasites and lose a few kilos in weight and I'm not as physically resilient as I was in my youth. When I arrived at the Congolese border this year, I experienced the usual sense of dread, wondering what sort of reception I would get from the immigration officials. Inexplicably, under another change in immigration policy it is again possible to get a visa for six nights at the border, but passports then have to be submitted at the Department of Immigration office in the city with an application, and extra fee, for all extensions. I wasn't too happy about relinquishing my passport but glad I had copies of the front pages I always carry with me.

***

In the village, I find people have almost finished building their stick-and-clay homes with materials provided by ADRA under instruction from the people I've paid. I strongly endorse Fred's policy, which is to help people help themselves. I've never thought it a good idea for well-meaning overseas volunteers to go in and take over work that can readily be done by locals. In labouring on the buildings, the people are learning skills to maintain their homes, and hopefully they will appreciate and take pride in ownership of the village.

Figure 4.2: Pygmies building their homes on their own land

Figure 4.3: Kinubi using hand tools to dig through lava rocks for a pit-toilet

We're welcomed enthusiastically as we drive into the village. Some of the houses need more clay and I authorise payment for another load to be brought in. I notice little Kinubi working behind his house, a young man who barely comes up to my shoulder. The muscles on his arms strain as he uses a few simple hand tools to excavate lumps of lava rock and make a deep hole for a pit-toilet. The rectangular houses, each on a 20-square-metre plot, are of the same standard as the dwellings of local tribes: two rooms with two windows and a door. They have been laid out with enough room around each house for individual latrines and a kitchen garden to be established. I realise that all the huts I see in Rwanda and Congo are rectangular rather than the round dwellings featured in the books about Africa that I saw as a child. It reminds me that Africa is a continent of different nations and I should be careful about assuming similarities of culture and worldview that aren't there.

I discover more of the history of this group of Pygmies and meet an elderly couple, Seseti and Zaina. Almost everyone in the village is descended from them. Seseti led the group out of the forest but now his son and nephew are in an uneasy truce, sharing the leadership. This day, the nephew Alexis is off on business of his own and it is the son, Mubawa, who is in charge. I authorise funds for him to buy banana roots and an assortment of avocado, mango and citrus trees for the gardens.

Figure 4.4: With Seseti and Zaina, from whom most of the people in the village are descended

Earlier in the year, Fabien had rented fertile land some distance from the camp where the Pygmies were still living and given them cabbage and cassava seedlings to plant there. Some of the women had laboured through the dry season, walking back and forth to the field every day – most of them with a babe on their back and some with a toddler by their side, too. But just when the cabbages were ready, one day they arrived to find someone had harvested and stolen the entire crop overnight.

Sympathetic friends in Australia have donated enough funds for nine of these women to receive a grant of $50 each so that they can set up some small enterprise and generate ongoing income for their family. We meet in Vumilia's house and each woman presents me with her business plan. The small enterprises range from raising chickens or ducks for eggs to using local fruits to make juice. Since the village is near the main highway to Sake, they plan to sit by the road and sell their products to passing travellers. Vumilia's interesting plan is to buy a pushbike for her husband Ferdie to ride the seven kilometres to the edge of the forest and buy a big bag of charcoal. They can divide the contents into smaller quantities which she will sell at a profit at Sake market.

Making sure no one is peering in the door I pass out a US$50 note for every woman and they carefully fold over the material at the waist of their *kanga* (skirt) and tuck it securely away. I realise I never see anyone with anything resembling a handbag so this is how they carry essential items. While Pygmies in the forest worked with bark and special grasses to make clothing, now the women wear the same outfits as all the local tribeswomen: mostly just a T-shirt and a length of brightly coloured and patterned cotton material wrapped around them for a skirt. This material often has writing on it – a proverb or Bible verse. They usually have a second piece of differently patterned material which can serve many purposes: it can be an apron, a basket, a shawl for rainy or cold weather, a way to attach their babies to their back. For special occasions, it is folded creatively to provide a magnificent headdress.

At the end of the meeting, Vumilia takes my hand and escorts me out of her house. 'I didn't believe you when you told us a year ago you would be back to help us,' she says, 'but you kept your word.' I wonder how many times she has been disappointed in her life and I recommit my aid to her people.

As we walk around the village, Fred shares some of the problems he has encountered. Early on in the project, Jules, one of the most cooperative of the leading Pygmy men, was standing on the back of a lorry bringing in clay from a place called Mitumbala for the walls of the houses. There is no clay around this area of Mubambiro – just lava rocks, gravel and dust. As the truck jolted unexpectedly on the uneven ground Jules fell off, hit his head and died instantly. The police became involved and it looked like the community would have to stop building. However, Jules' family refused to prosecute. Fred told me, 'His family said we know this is for our benefit and our brother would not want to cause problems for you when you are helping us.' I pay a visit to the home of the dead man's brother and his young wife who just yesterday gave birth to their first child. As discreetly as possible I hand over US$50 as a form of compensation for their loss.

Some of the houses are further ahead than others. Rose has painted a rose on the front of her house and someone has written the French *Merci*. Nyota, which means 'star', has drawn a star on her house and someone has written in Swahili, 'When God lifts me up how amazed everyone is.' ADRA has also provided a mattress, a blanket, simple cooking pots and a lamp for every household: more possessions than these people have ever enjoyed.

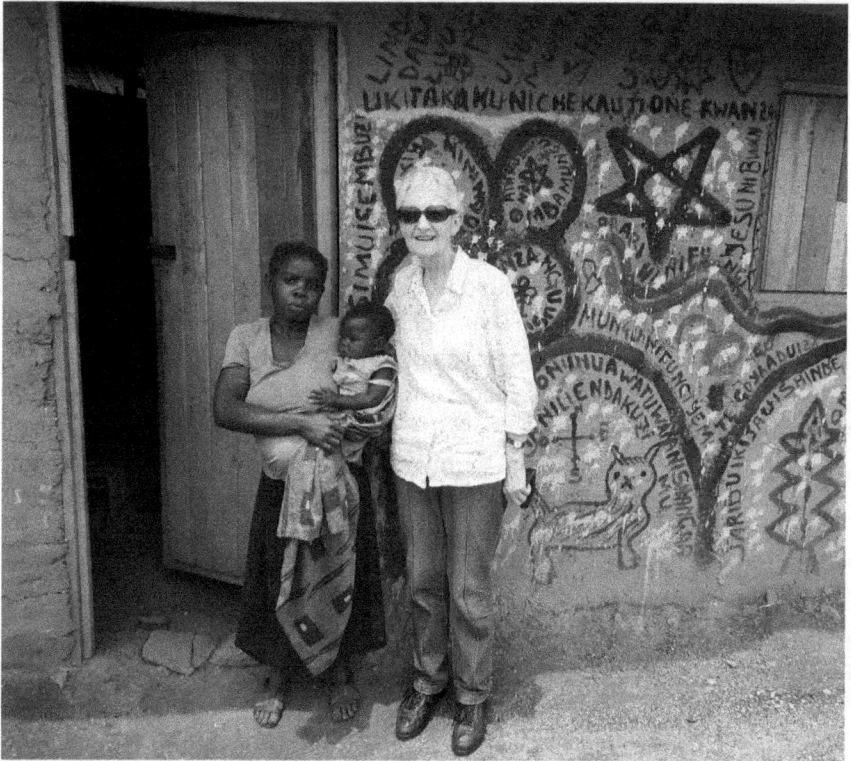

Figure 4.5: Nyota, which means 'star', drew a star on her house

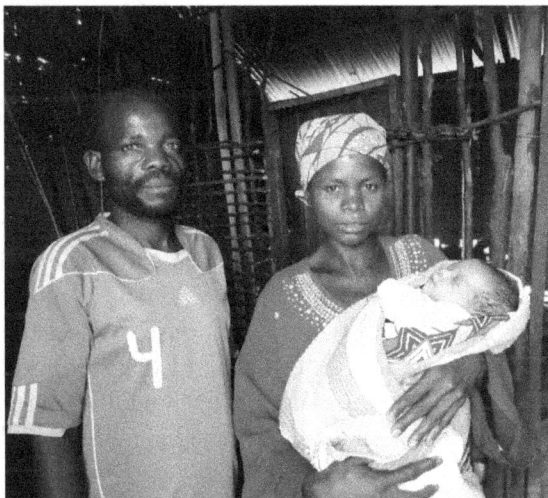

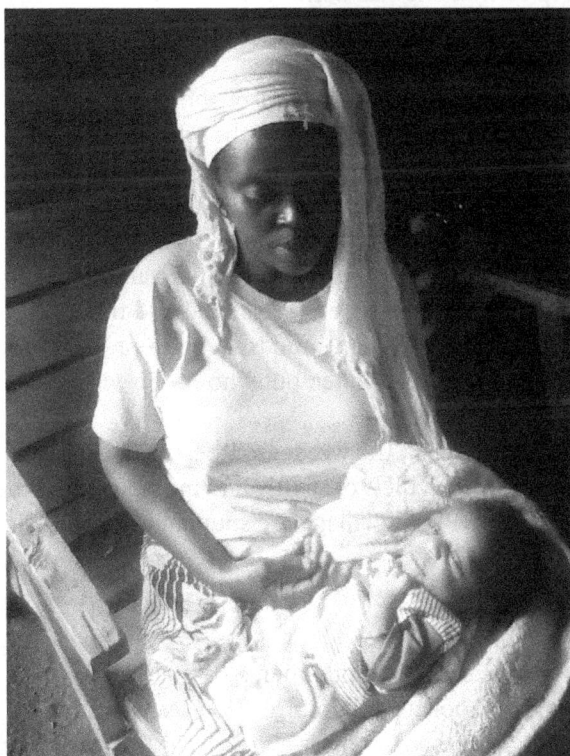

Figure 4.6 and 4.7: New-born babies in the village

Suddenly, people are shouting and Fabien is called away to assist a woman who is giving birth and in distress. I know that in March when this woman was five months pregnant, she was raped on the verge of the forest where she was gathering nuts and roots to feed her five hungry children. Fabien returns at last to inform us she has safely given birth to a healthy boy. He will be named after Fabien in gratitude for his help. Fabien was once chief theatre nurse at HEAL Africa Hospital and he always carries a surgical scalpel with him in anticipation of having to attend a birth and sever the umbilical cord, which otherwise would be cut with a none-too-clean sharp stone.

I'm invited to go into the house to meet the new little Fabien. It's the first time I've seen a newborn in Congo. Shocked, I ask Fabien if this pale-skinned babe is the child of rape by a European. He laughingly explains that it can take several days for the pigment in black skin to take effect: the child is pure *Mbuti*.

The new mother indicates that she has some pain and I pull out my supply of paracetamol. There are eight tablets left and I ask Fabien to ensure she knows the correct dosage. For safe-keeping she tucks the tablets between the sticks that make up the supports for the walls of the clay hut. I ask about circumcision and they tell me that the elders in the village circumcise teenage boys in an age-old ritual, but of course it's men's business and no one will say any more about it. They do share the information that circumcision or genital mutilation of girls, once considered a way to prevent promiscuity, has been outlawed. I ask if the birth will be registered officially. Tuteene has told me that many Pygmies have never been registered and this causes problems when they try to enrol at school. If a child isn't registered within a short time after birth there is a fee to do so later, but who in this village has spare cash to do that?

As we drive away after this first visit, the wet season begins in earnest. I watch the tropical downpour create rivulets of swiftly flowing water and I'm thankful that all the babies in the Pygmy village are snug and dry in their new houses.

***

In Congo the school year begins in early September, so a major task every trip is to enrol the children in school at Mubambiro. This year we enrolled a total of sixty-six children in primary and junior high school and provided all of them with the required uniform, plastic sandals, books and bags. We bought out the contents of one small store after another in the street of shoes because none of the shops stocked enough in the required sizes. In junior high the children had the option of studying health, agriculture or 'electricity' as their elective. Eric and Heritier had chosen health as their elective but our high achiever, Dieudonne, had chosen electricity. Principal Anselm told me that this was no longer possible because the essential teaching aid, the school's generator, was worn out. Samuel scoured Goma to find a generator to replace it. Given all the extras I was providing for the school I wasn't happy that school fees had risen and now I was paying $100 for primary students and $200 for those in high school. I was also suspicious that not all of the eight children I was supporting in high school were in fact Pygmies. Anselm admitted that some of the children were orphans from his local tribe – and how could I abandon them!

After I'd paid the school fees we went to visit the local Bantu village and the ramshackle timber cabin Anselm had rented to house the preschool children. I was informed it was used as a church on Sundays. Inside it was dark and windowless with an uneven dirt floor. There was a limit to what the teachers could do with the children, both inside and outside the building, where it was too hot in the dry season and too wet and muddy in the wet season. It was an unsafe and unhealthy environment. The staff were keeping order with a stick in hand, which they didn't hesitate to use on the little children. Zico had once mentioned that children know teachers really care about them when they use a stick to beat them and help them pay attention in class, but I didn't want this to continue with these children. I had brought with me a French language video of a preschool in France, so I invited the teachers to Goma for a day to view it and do some rudimentary training about alternative methods of discipline. Whether or not this would convince them to change their methods remained to be seen.

The visit to the preschool site was added incentive for me to build a community centre, an idea that had been taking shape in my mind. If we had a substantial building it would allow us to do so much more for the villagers. It would serve as a place for community meetings, for the preschool children in the mornings and a place for holding sewing and other classes in the afternoon. Fabien could hold pre-natal classes and a clinic to treat the minor illnesses which, given the poor nutrition of the villagers, so often proved deadly. I'd nearly passed out from fatigue and heat one day, so from my point of view it would also be wonderful if there was a place where I could sit and rest during the long days in Mubambiro.

Another project that could take place in a community centre came to my attention. A young woman called Evelyn who had recently returned to the village and was staying with her uncle, Mubawa, came up and introduced herself to me. She'd been taken to HEAL Africa Hospital for the birth of a son some years before, and Lyn, recognising her potential, had arranged for her to go to a program in South Kivu where she was trained to teach literacy. She was already holding classes for some of the women in Mubawa's house, but could do so much more if we had a suitable building.

Convinced of the worth of providing a multipurpose centre for the village, I consulted with Joseph, the architect who had worked on the houses, and within a day he had drawn up plans for a building in lava rock bricks, with lots of windows and an office at one end. Quite unexpectedly, an ideal position for this project suddenly became available in the village, close to the road and easily accessed by all residents. When we'd secured the land in 2010, Maitre Martin had registered it in the names of all the Pygmy heads of families selected for resettlement by Fred. Fred had warned me that in other ADRA projects, people had removed their roofs and sold the sheets of iron. I couldn't blame people for exchanging their only asset for cash in certain circumstances, for example if a child was in need of life-saving medical care. But from the start we had made it clear to the Pygmy villagers that they could not sell their house, the roof or the land. We were feeding the children, providing medical care for everyone and in the event of a legitimate need for emergency cash we could be relied upon to help. So I was very disappointed to discover that already one of the Pygmy families had sold their house to a woman from the local tribe. As far as the group of Bantu men who were helping me could ascertain, there was no good reason. We called a meeting and decided that to prevent others doing this, we needed to be ruthless and tear down the house. The woman who had bought the hut was furious, but she had known all along that the land and houses were exclusively for the Pygmies who were named on the legal documents. It was a harsh lesson for all involved but the removal of the house gave us a perfect site for a community centre.

Finally, as we discussed the use of the proposed building, some of the women raised the need for a church. They had told me on my first visit that they wanted a place to worship, but there were so many pressing practical needs at the time that I couldn't respond. In fact, their request back then had come as a surprise to me. I had heard the Pygmies described as animists, and the old people in the village had told me that their 'god' was the Forest, now lost to them. Obviously, since leaving the deep forest they had been exposed to Christianity. Some 80 per cent of Congolese identify as Christian, a legacy of the colonisation by Belgium. Driving around Goma on previous visits I'd been amazed at the plethora of churches, the names on the buildings all indicating a different version of Christianity. Samuel, who now accompanied me everywhere as interpreter and guide, responded to my questions about this: 'People in your country have many material supports when you face troubles so you don't need God like we do.' On the other hand, he also warned me about the way religion was used by some people. Commanders of some of the rebel militias proclaimed themselves prophets of God and sanctioned merciless attacks on defenceless civilians to terrify the population into submission, all in the name of Christ. When people not only don't have Bibles, but don't know how to read anyway, powerful men have always twisted Christ's message of love, unity and peace to suit their own ends.

For the Pygmy village, clearly the proposed building could easily double as a place of worship on Sundays. While thinking about this project I remembered meeting a man called Thomson in one of the HAH workshops. He had mentioned that he worked with a development project for Pygmies settled south of Goma which was funded by the Anglican Katindo Church in Goma where he was a lay preacher. I contacted him and asked if he would consider visiting Mubambiro on Sundays to hold a service for them once we had a building and if I paid his travel expenses. He was so enthusiastic that an open-air service was planned for the following weekend. Most of the Pygmies turned up, and also many people from the local tribes and families of the military in the nearby camp. The church service could be one way of integrating the Pygmies with the local population. The challenge for me when I got back to Australia would be to find the $20 000 required for the building.

With so much happening in the village I was hoping that in Munguiko, who had passed the State Finals Examination in June as predicted, the village would have an educated leader. Certainly, he was the first Pygmy to do so in this region and among the very small percentage of the general population in Congo who had even as much as three years of education. We made arrangements for him to continue his education at the university in Goma, initially living in a small hut on Fabien's property. Kayese had failed the State Finals but he had been sick with a bout of malaria at the time of sitting for the examination so I agreed to pay the fees for him to repeat the year and try again next June.

Eager for Munguiko to take his place as a leader of the village, I planned for him to be involved in the management of the programs. I'd had a costly lesson last year. I'd left it to the interpreter, who had previously worked so diligently and so well with me, to open an account at a bank in Goma, and I'd deposited $6000. But he had disappeared and so had the money. His relatives in Australia had warned me about him, but it was a lesson I had to learn the hard way. When we work with communities in which life is so precarious and abject poverty ever-present, those of us from affluent nations like Australia need to ensure that we don't set up situations where people might be tempted to steal. For people in such dire circumstances, the immediate gains outweigh negative future consequences which in an uncertain environment may never happen.

With our lawyer's help, we set up a new account in Maitre Martin's name, but I intended that withdrawals require the signatures of at least two of three other men: Samuel, Fabien and Munguiko. But Munguiko arrived late for the appointment at the bank and without the identity card we had arranged for him, so could not be included. It was disappointing, but I accepted that it would take time for him to grow into the responsible leader I was hoping for.

Although the week was passing so quickly, Fred, Fabien and Samuel were all keen for me to visit Kitshanga, a region about 120 kilometres from Goma. Samuel's in-laws came from this region and Fabien wanted to meet Pygmy communities camping in the area. When Tuteene heard about this trip he opted out, telling me it wasn't safe. However, I felt there was good reason to meet the other Pygmy groups and I didn't want to miss the opportunity to see more of this incredibly beautiful country.

We set off early in the day and made a brief stop at a pretty rural centre called Shasha to visit an HAH sewing project for rape survivors, part of the Women Stand Up Together recovery and empowerment program. I met some of the women who had found support from associating with other rape survivors, not in order to repeat their trauma stories but to encourage one another in a journey towards healing and independence. Once we were back on the road to Kitshanga, Fred pointed over the side of the mountain we were rounding to a lush green valley. 'My native village. I was born there and my father and all the generations before me,' he said. I couldn't see any sign of a village. 'No one lives there now,' he agreed, 'it is not safe.'

Later, Samuel pointed out another deserted area called Kirolirwe. He told me it was where an HAH counsellor's family, along with seven hundred other families, were massacred by the Rwandan army as they swept across the border in July 1996 in a preview of the later conflict that became 'the Great African War' involving nine nations. He recalled that his younger brother had been staying in that village. Warned of the danger that was imminent, Samuel hastened to get there in time to take his brother to safety in Goma. The two boys escaped the village less than an hour ahead of the invading troops, and as they fled on foot they could hear the distant gunfire that went on for hours on that dreadful day.

The further we travelled, the more splendid the scenery was, with villages barely visible, nestled in among the vegetation on the hillsides. We went through heavily forested areas and then past postcard-perfect vistas of rolling hills cleared of vegetation and given over to pasture for herds of cattle. It all looked so peaceful, but Fred told me that the fertile fields where food crops had fed many Congolese had been taken over by Rwandans who were pastoralists rather than farmers. A lot of the time I couldn't follow the conversation. The men were speaking in the usual mixture of French and Swahili that confused me. In any case, I was thrown about with every jerk and jolt of the vehicle on the unsealed, rain-slicked road and was preoccupied with trying to stay upright.

I did notice a small military post we passed and didn't recognise the flag flying out front. I tapped Samuel on the shoulder and asked him what it was. He hadn't been paying attention but our driver had. What he said had an electrifying effect on the other men and there was an animated exchange between them. At last Samuel turned to me, 'Well, that is the flag of one of the Rwandan militia, but don't worry, we are sure they are a political group now, not engaged in terrorism.' He didn't explain, but I assumed they were the Tutsi-backed National Congress for Defence of the People (CNDP), which I knew had only recently come to an agreement with the Congolese Government to cease armed combat. I huddled back in the vehicle and fervently hoped they were not their opponents, the Hutu Democratic Forces for the Liberation of Rwanda (FDLR), the men who were responsible for atrocities in Rwanda and now in Congo. These two militia had been fighting a proxy war in Eastern Congo with the Congolese as collateral damage.

It took us more than three hours to get to the area where Fabien expected to find the group of Pygmies he had heard about. We were all hungry so snacked on freshly cooked corn on the cob at a roadside stall. I'm usually wary of eating outside the guesthouse, but since the juicy corn was cooked in its outer leaves and I was very hungry I relented. As a rule, I never ate or drank in a village where starving people might see me unless I had food enough to share.

We had to get out of the car and climb a steep and slippery hillside in the light but penetrating drizzle to reach the Pygmy camp. Their circumstances were beyond miserable. From a scatter of pitiful grass shelters the ragged group of men, women and children emerged to greet us. Fred asked me if I recognised the smell coming from one of the grass humpies, but it wasn't until I noticed the marijuana plants growing around the camp that I realised they were preparing the freshly harvested leaves by smoking them in the hut. Fred said they used it themselves to deaden their awareness of the cold and their hunger. Although it was illegal to do so, they were able to sell or exchange some for necessities if they were careful to avoid the attention of the police. We questioned the wizened old leader, who told us that, like our friends at Mubambiro, these Pygmies had been wandering from place to place for more than a generation since leaving the forest. However, they had high hopes that the local chief here was planning to offer them some good land nearby to settle on. That was until last night, when there had been action down in the valley we had just driven through and the chief had been killed.

Fabien took note of the number of people and especially the children. He was planning to put in a proposal to a European aid agency for funds to set up a vocational training program for rape survivors, Pygmies and rehabilitated child soldiers. I saw some adults take an interest in the conversation, hope dawning on their faces. But although I was so moved by their story, for my part I knew I couldn't promise any help for these people. I had learnt in my eight years working in South Vietnam that it is unwise to extend a program of aid too widely and too quickly. These people were too far from Goma and my trusted assistants. When everyone is struggling to survive, the temptation is too great for unsupervised local staff to misuse funds to maximise their own benefit.

Figure 4.8: I couldn't help the Pygmy band at Kitshanga

There had been so much to do out at the new village in Mubambiro in the first week of my stay that as soon as I recovered from the long trip to Kitshanga I organised the workshop for HAH staff working with traumatised children. On my previous trip to Congo in February, I'd selected four women from among the counsellors who were interested and motivated to meet with a group of traumatised children and explore the usefulness of a form of therapy that had been developed in South Africa. The program engaged children in art and dance and used the analogy of the life of a tree to help them move on from traumatic events in their lives. It was designed to encourage children to view their current situation from a place of strength and safety rather than as helpless victims.

I hired the grounds of the Bungwe to conduct the three-day workshop under a marquee on the lawn amid palm trees, flowering bushes and huge ornamental avocado trees – a perfect background for the activities. The gardener continued his painstaking work around us, squatting to trim the lawn with a pair of clippers. It occurred to me that even if a lawnmower could be found in Goma, given the level of unemployment in the city it was to his advantage to make this a full-time job. The counsellors led the program for eight children whose guardians agreed for them to participate. All of the children were orphans or fatherless as a result of the conflict. Three little girls were part of HAH's program for children who were HIV positive. I'd visited their homes back in 2009 because their education was being sponsored by my friends at St Mark's Anglican Church at South Hurstville in Sydney. One child lived with her grandmother, who was also HIV positive, and the entire family of one of the others was HIV positive. I'd met with them all each visit so far and noted the deterioration in the health of the adults responsible for these children. Apparently the essential antiretroviral medications, once donated for adults by European agencies, were no longer available because of the Global Financial Crisis. I wondered what would happen to the children if these people died. As for the boys, one had seen his father tortured to death; another had been mute since his parents were killed in his presence.

At the end of the program, I was moved to tears by the responses of the children when they spoke about their hopes for the future. The most confronting moment was when the boy who hadn't spoken in months held up his drawing of an aircraft and spoke for the first time. Samuel interpreted for me. 'I hope to become a pilot.' But then added the chilling conclusion. 'In a plane I will hunt down and kill the soldiers who killed my parents.'

Chapter 5

Love and forgiveness – September 2012

Arriving in the village we are mobbed and applauded as always, even though I've asked Samuel to tell people they need not do this. Mubawa has a group of children assembled and I'm embarrassed as I recognise they are singing in Swahili, 'Mama Barbara, we love you, mother of the Pygmies'. I wonder again how I can live up to their expectations of me. I'm glad when Vumilia takes my hand and leads me to her home for the meeting we've planned with the women who were given the income-generating grants on my last visit.

The little hut is overcrowded. Vumilia opens the wooden shutters on the windows to let in light and air, and arranges stools and a couple of lava rocks for all of us to have a seat. She indicates a new feature in the house for me to admire. She has divided the main room off from the sleeping area with a lace curtain, material that I recognise came from a bag full of remnants a friend in Australia had donated last year. Each woman has a small child or two with her and it takes a while for everyone to settle down. I notice that Jacquie, one of the women who received the $50 grant twelve months ago, has not yet arrived. I ask if she knows we are meeting and they exchange glances before they reply, 'She died.' Reluctantly they add, 'She was cursed by a woman who is a witch.' Jacquie's death and the news that there's a witch in the village come as a shock. 'Who can that be?' I wonder. Pragmatically, Samuel gets on with the purpose of the meeting: reports on the progress the women have made in developing a source of income.

Figure 5.1: Women meeting to report on the income-generating grants

71

Figure 5.2: Ferdie and Vumilia with their bicycle

Ferdie, Vumilia's husband, has already shown me the bicycle they decided to buy with the grant last year. He has set off to Sake market to work as a one-man delivery service for people who can't carry their own purchases. I've seen the way these pushbikes are loaded up and pity this man who is an important role-model for other men in the village, especially the younger men who tend to hang around the village with nothing to do. As planned, when Ferdie saves up enough cash from deliveries, he goes to the forest edge and buys a 50-kilogram bag of charcoal, an essential for cooking in every household in the region as there is no power. He takes it back to the village for Vumilia to divide the charcoal into smaller quantities, which she sells at a profit in Sake market to people who can't afford to buy in bulk. For all this effort, he told me they make a profit of about US$7 a week.

Nathalie has had some success selling a type of cake at the side of the road. I have tried the cake – just once was enough. It is made of cassava flour, fried in oil with no sugar. Irene makes a pittance buying sugarcane, cutting it into small pieces and selling it to children outside the schools. Colette has had the most success with her 'banana juice' project – the juice is apparently very popular with the men in the village as well as the locals. The women are giggling to one another and I ask Samuel for an explanation. The 'juice' is actually fermented bananas or yams, which make an intoxicating beer.

Mamisa's report is up next. She has bought a breeding goat but is still waiting for the goat to give birth, and is hoping for twins. Shu Krani also bought a goat and is pleased to announce it has given birth. I had expected that the goats might provide milk for the children, but Samuel explains that the goats must survive on roadside weeds, and on such inadequate feed they don't give much milk. The reason for raising these animals is to sell the offspring to people who will want them to offer as a bride price or for sacrifices for health and safety. Siwa, Bwema and Nyota confess they have little to show for their efforts. They too had decided to buy livestock – chickens and ducks, two piglets and a couple of goats – but they tell me all the poultry died when a sickness went through the village during the wet season. I think to myself that people who often only have cabbage leaves to eat themselves might find it hard to share them with birds. Perhaps it was too much of a temptation to kill the poultry and eat them instead? The pigs are still alive, but growing quickly and living in the house with the children. Samuel makes a note for a carpenter to come and build a pigsty.

I understand why some of the women have spent a portion of the grant on food or medicines. I suspect that only Vumilia gets much support from her husband. The reports completed, Samuel decides to broach a difficult subject with the women: the danger to their health and to the children when they give birth almost every year. While birth control is no longer officially illegal in Congo, the idea is still unacceptable to most people, and in any case, none of these people can afford to buy any sort of contraceptive. Samuel's attempts to introduce the subject are met with gales of embarrassed laughter. But in serious vein, Vumilia admits the women all wish they had some control in this matter – it is the men in their lives who make any sort of restraint impossible. What else is there for the men to do at night but make babies! And in their circumstances they have good reason to have many children. At least three in ten of the children in the village die before they are five years old, and since there is no pension and no welfare system, people need to have some surviving children to look after them in old age. And it is obvious that the men do love their children!

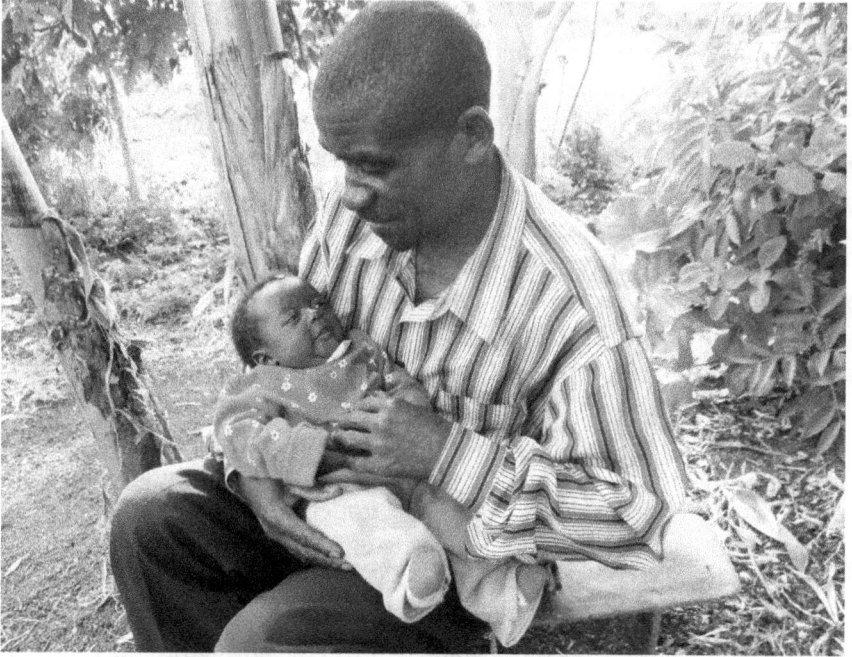

Figure 5.3: Grandfather Bertin, leader of the other extended family in the village, adores his latest grandchild

Before our meeting ends, Vumilia makes a small speech, thanking me and the friends in faraway Australia who care enough to send funds to help people they don't know. Then Colette comes from the back of the house with a splendid live rooster and puts him in my lap where he makes himself comfortable. I'm overwhelmed. I know a hen costs about $8 – how can they afford this? And then a terrible thought comes into my head unbidden: bird flu has killed poultry around the world this year. Is this what carried off the chickens and ducks, and is this poor creature likely to infect me?

***

I arrived in Goma this trip after months of uncertainty. It is twelve months now since my last visit. I had intended to come back six months ago, but I had a fall at Christmas 2011 getting out of sea baths with a two-year-old child in my arms. He was the son of a Congolese family in Sydney, one of several Congolese families who gathered with me for a picnic at the beach near my home one Sunday. According to 2011 figures, less than three thousand Congolese have been granted refugee status and now live in Australia. Most are still struggling to find their feet. They do send money home to family, like all refugee and immigrant communities, but in Congo their limited assistance can only help with survival needs and doesn't lift people out of poverty.

It was a fun occasion on a warm sunny day, and while the adults chatted over the food, I was with a dozen or so of the children in the water. Little John, who had never been to a beach before, clung to me like a leech on one side, while the elderly grandmother of one family, fully dressed, clutched at me on the other. We were unprepared when a rogue wave hit, sending us under the water. Grandma came up spluttering, and never having been in sea water before she couldn't understand why it tasted so bad!

I twisted my knee badly getting up after the fall, and that problem and reports of an upsurge of violence in Congo convinced me to postpone my next trip back to Goma. Throughout the first seven to eight months of 2012, messages from my friends and advisers who I called the 'Good Men of Congo', and rare reports in the international media, recorded the increasing level of violence in the provinces of North and South Kivu. From the south, Tuteene sent horrific photos of fifty-six people in the Pygmy village at Kamanaga who were massacred one night. The photographs of little children hacked to death as they slept broke my heart. I sent what I could for him to help the survivors as he had taken in twenty orphans to live in his house. He said none of the international agencies had offered any help at all.

In North Kivu province, dozens of militia bands were not only fighting the Congolese Army but outdoing each other in committing atrocities, burning homes, and shooting hundreds of helpless civilians as they fled. These militias included the Mai Mai (a type of civilian defence force formed by different tribes to protect their own interests against other tribes) and the two rival rebel groups with ties to Rwanda. Many settlements between Goma and Kitshanga where I'd travelled last September had since been abandoned to the rebels as Congolese government soldiers fled. I heard that two thousand five hundred Pygmies had been caught up in the wave of refugees and wondered if the people I had met at Kitshanga were among them. In both May and June, Tuteene reported he personally knew of one hundred Pygmy women who had been raped in the chaos.

In July 2012, the BBC announced that the Movement of March 23 (M23), a new, well-organised rebel militia, possibly armed by Rwanda, was maybe ten kilometres from Mubambiro. Samuel told me the Pygmy men of the village had decided to stay and try to protect their homes while the women and children fled on foot down the highway and joined 750 000 refugees in Goma and in camps at Nsulo and Mugunga on Goma's outskirts. Some armed men did briefly enter the village and looted the houses of the mattresses and whatever else they could carry off, but there was no loss of life or major destruction. A political solution was reached and in the uneasy peace our friends drifted back home to the village.

So in early September I made this, my fifth trip. I left Australia with a thankful heart because some unexpected and generous gifts had come in just days before my departure and I had the $20 000 needed for the construction of a substantial building to serve as a community centre. I thought it might also be a place of refuge if the village should come under attack in the future – especially for the women and children. More than half the funds for the building had already been transferred to the bank in Congo.

My priority on arriving in Goma was to get the building under way, and Samuel and I went out to Mubambiro without delay. Security on the road was certainly tighter than in previous years. Every day our papers were demanded and the vehicle searched for weapons at least four times on the way to and coming back from Mubambiro. The soldiers at the checkpoints usually asked me for cigarettes and my usual reply was to offer them a blessing in Swahili, *Mubarikiwe*, which they came to expect. The military camp close to the Pygmy village expanded daily as new recruits and their families arrived. I pitied them as they made their homes in shallow dugouts wherever there was a spare piece of ground, and covered them over with pieces of canvas, straw mats or whatever they could improvise for a roof.

With a steering committee of the Good Men of Congo and engineer Jean Bizi from HAH, I met with Joseph, our architect/builder. He had been the architect for the village, and he and the Pygmies knew each other. He would be able to choose willing workers to help with the labour. We decided on the site and the plans, drew up the contract, approved the materials, and confirmed the budget and schedule for completing the project. Dr Jo, director of HAH, authorised our use of a nearby hospital warehouse to store the lava bricks, cement, iron bars and roofing materials securely during construction. The relevant traditional and district chiefs didn't keep appointments we made, but I managed to catch them unexpectedly at various places in the region to gain their cooperation, and they all turned up for the dedication and ground-breaking ceremony.

One day as I walked around the village, people pointed out the shallow grave behind her house where Jacquie had been buried. When they told me that burial close to the house was the norm when anyone died, I wondered about the implications for the health of the population. I could think of no alternative solution to the problem. Inspecting the banana and fruit trees planted last year, I was pleased to see some were flourishing despite the poor soil. As I passed the house of Seseti and Zaina, the patriarch and matriarch of the people, Seseti stepped out and greeted me. He had resigned his role as leader, but he continued to impress me with his initiative and foresight. He indicated a plot of seedling eucalyptus trees he had managed to raise just outside his house and asked me to help organise for them to be transplanted at Nyabirere, where land had been given to the group by the traditional high chief some years ago. While Nyabirere was unsafe for establishing a village, he was certain the trees could flourish there untended. Eucalyptus saplings had been bought and brought in to form the frames for the clay and cement daub houses when the village had been established. In future years when the houses might need to be repaired or rebuilt, these trees would be ready for use.

We hired a truck in Sake, loaded the seedlings and tools, and set off for Nyabirere. The sky was overcast, the sparse vegetation as dark as the black lava dust of the ground. As we came to a stop not far from the road, I had a sense of foreboding and menace I'd never experienced in any of the remote locations I'd visited in the past. Tuteene, in his brown costume that day, jumped down from our vehicle enthusiastic about other potential uses of the land, but I decided to stay out of sight in the truck. It wasn't until the seedlings were planted and we were on the road with the men back on the truck that I felt safe again. I'd heard too many stories about people being kidnapped for ransom and I feared that, as a white woman, I would be an irresistible target for armed men who might be hovering in the shadows of the surrounding countryside.

***

With the new school year about to start there were hard decisions to be made about who could be sponsored. The construction costs for the new building meant there would be less funds for school fees. In the end, I paid for forty-five primary school and seven junior high places. The payment included fees for Florence, the only girl from the Pygmy village who had successfully completed primary school, and the four Pygmy boys Eric, Heritier, Dieudonne and a younger boy called Mustafa who were all making good progress in junior high despite the disruption to classes during the height of the recent conflict. Kayese had failed the State Finals Examinations again but begged for another chance since his school had been closed for most of the time in the months prior to the examinations in June. Munguiko had abandoned his studies at the university even before he had really begun. Although only eighteen years old he already had a wife and baby, and his wife was pregnant again. He pleaded that he had to be back with her when the security situation deteriorated. It made sense to me. Life is so unpredictable here that people cannot commit unconditionally to any responsibility outside their family. I also suspected he had found the discrimination that Pygmies usually experience hard to take when he was on his own in the city.

At the preschool I was surprised to find that Nsii had been replaced as principal by Nicole, who had recently given birth. After my workshop with the teachers on creative play, Nsii found Samuel and me in a secluded area of the village and in floods of tears explained what had happened. Anselm, in her words, wanted her to 'love him'. When she refused, he threatened to dismiss her altogether but because that would mean he would lose one share of the wages I was paying the six women, he merely demoted her. I had no idea that he was withholding money from the women and wondered why they hadn't complained. Then she revealed that Nicole was actually his wife, two of the other teachers were his sisters, and the teacher's aide was his mother.

Anselm had no shame when confronted with such blatant nepotism. Reluctantly, I paid the women off with a month's wages, reinstated Nsii, and Sylvie, Anselm's most able sister, and also hired the Pygmy woman Evelyn, who was making such a success of the literacy classes. It was another lesson in the different worldview of people living in such an unpredictable, chaotic situation. Foreigners are fair game; nepotism is normal; first obligation is to family and then tribe. Foreigners may never come back so why worry about the consequences of illegal actions that may never come to light.

***

Although by now the projects for the Pygmies at Mubambiro were the focus of my work in Congo, my association with HEAL Africa Hospital continued. Dr Jo still provided the essential letter of invitation without which I could not have entered the country. This year, though, there had been no reunion with Lyn. That amazing British woman who'd spent forty years of her life helping the women of Congo had died of cancer on 17 March 2012. The staff told me the people of Goma mourned her for a week. The local radio stations played hymns all day long in her memory. The city authorities renamed a street leading to the hospital after her and it is one of the few partially sealed roads in the city. My last conversation with her was before she knew she had outlived the months of reprieve that prayer and the best possible treatment in the United Kingdom had given her. At that time, she told me she had no fear of dying and no regrets. Her life had been so full and so satisfying and she knew the hospital would continue to serve the people of North Kivu. Dr Jo was from the Nande tribe whose traditional lands are north of Goma in the city of Beni, and she had chosen to be buried there in the soil of Congo.

I spoke twice at the hospital chapel service, assuring the staff and patients that they were not forgotten by my friends and supporters in Australia. I taught them words and action to the children's chorus about God's love, 'Wide, wide as the ocean', but in the middle of the translation realised that none of them in this landlocked nation had ever seen the seashore from a distance, let alone been near the ocean, and it would be better to refer to Lake Kivu, although that comparison was completely inadequate to convey the boundless love of God for all creation. I was disappointed that the *a cappella* singing had been replaced by electronic instruments with the microphones so loud my ears hurt.

***

For the psychosocial counsellors, I had an idea for one final follow-up seminar on the topic of forgiveness. I knew that they routinely advised survivors of rape torture that in the interests of their own mental health they should forgive the men who had assaulted them. Moreover, most of the staff and the patients who came to this hospital were at least nominally Christian and familiar with the prayer, 'Forgive us our sins as we forgive those who sin against us'. When I opened up this subject for discussion, one of the counsellors had a lot to say about the difficulty rape survivors might have with forgiving those who had sinned against them. She had been raped when she was just thirteen years old and as a result had given birth to twin daughters. It wasn't just the rapist she couldn't forgive. She blamed her parents for not protecting her and the children who, by their very existence, she felt had ruined her life. Men looked on her as damaged goods, possibly infected with HIV, and not good wife material. She had also had to abandon her studies and her dreams of earning a university degree. 'How can I forgive God for letting this happen to me?' she asked.

The other participants nodded. It was a question they often had to field. And her candid revelation opened the gates to a flood of stories of unforgivable cruelty. I can't repeat some and wish I could forget them. One woman in the group told how her husband had thrown her and their two-year-old daughter out of her home when she was semi-paralysed and helpless after the botched delivery of her second child. I had already visited the HAH village Grounds for Hope for women in this situation and those who were outcasts because the extensive internal damage inflicted in their rape could not be repaired. Another participant told of a patient who had tried to run away from a band of soldiers who surprised her on the forest verge where she had gone to harvest nuts she could sell to pay for her son's school fees. After violently raping her, the soldiers broke her leg. They said it was just punishment since they were far from their wives protecting her village and yet she denied them the sex they needed. (I've heard that some soldiers think that sex protects them in battle.) They left her to die at the edge of the forest and only the perseverance of her children in finding her and getting her to the hospital saved her life.

Then there were the rape survivors from a remote village where all the men had been killed. The three women had been raped with sticks and they had brought the sticks with them to the hospital as evidence of the brutality they had endured. But everyone in the seminar agreed that almost without exception there is no justice for women. Men did as they pleased with impunity. Evidence disappeared from police reports. Women who dared to accuse members of the military had to face a military court in a military camp – an experience too daunting for most to even think about. Nor could women be sure that there would not be retribution for their testimony from the man's family and friends. And in any case, often there were many perpetrators, and women were so overwhelmed by terror at the time of the assault that they couldn't identify any of them. The counsellors said that for some women, the experience is too shameful to talk about, but in the right circumstances they poured out a jumble of mixed emotions: grief for the loss of a sense of security and control, anger mixed in with frustration, guilt and self-blame that they had not been able to avoid the assault. Like women across cultures and through the ages they were subjected to 'victim blaming' within their communities and even by their immediate families.

Eventually, the discussion moved on to acknowledge that forgiveness might be a process that takes time to achieve rather than something that happens immediately just because a woman is challenged to do so. We reviewed the BITS model I had introduced in the seminar in February 2011 and the value in survivors being able to forgive themselves and to recognise that the blame rested with the perpetrators; that forgiveness, when and if it became possible, was the survivor's gift and that it would come out of her own experience of being forgiven. After my work with the counselling staff over these past five visits I had more understanding of the difficulties they faced as well as the suffering of their clients. I was encouraged by the knowledge that there were now some effective practical and empowerment programs for women once they returned to their rural communities, such as Women Stand Up Together and Grounds for Hope. In these programs women challenged the common assumption that they were responsible for their assault and mobilised all women to protest about the impunity permitted to the perpetrators.

As in all of my seminars with the counsellors, we discussed ways for the staff to protect their own mental health given that their work involved hearing appalling stories on an almost daily basis. Some of the women recalled how an American visitor several years ago treated all the counsellors to a night at a luxury hotel on the lake. It was most therapeutic, they assured me. Especially for those who partied all night in the hotel pool – fully clothed.

Figure 5.4: With counsellors Prudence and Georgine in the hospital grounds, where new buildings have allowed the scope of the work to expand

In the village I learnt of another possible outcome of rape. One day a young Pygmy man came asking for a sizeable amount of money to pay the *mali* (bride price) for him to marry his sweetheart, who was Bantu from one of the nearby villages. I knew him already because he led a group of young men who always hung about our vehicle when I was there. Some time ago he'd wanted to form a soccer team so I'd provided T-shirts and a ball. At first, I didn't realise that the 'bride' was a stunningly beautiful young woman I'd often noticed because she stood head and shoulders above the other women and most of the men in our village. When I asked Samuel for advice about this request I was horrified to hear that this man had kidnapped and raped his 'bride'. He had spent time in prison for the rape, which had resulted in pregnancy, but was released when he promised her family he would marry her. I'd since learnt that in some cases of rape, this was a preferred outcome to spare both families the shame, but it was not necessarily in the best interests of the woman involved. I didn't give him the money, but I heard that the woman was living with him anyway, and safely delivered a child.

⁎⁎⁎

Since I'd discovered the Bungwe on my second Goma visit I'd continued to stay there. I was treated so well there that my friends called me the Princess of the Bungwe! Last year I'd noticed that while guests stayed in one of half a dozen bungalows, each of which had several rooms with en suite, there was one smaller building which consisted of a single bedroom with en suite and a tiny sitting room. This year I'd reserved this 'apartment' as it was called. It was a relief to have a private space to work in rather than conducting meetings and preparing for seminars in the busy dining-room.

Despite this relative luxury, I was weary as I crossed the border into Rwanda at the end of the trip and climbed into Deo's car to begin the long drive to Kigali airport. I reflected on all that had happened in the past years. I knew I could never have achieved so much without the help of the Good Men of Congo. In a country where many men behaved with such ferocious cruelty to others, especially women and children, it was reassuring to know men like Samuel, Fabien, Fred, Martin and Tuteene. It had been hard to say goodbye to them at the border, but I knew I would be back.

Figure 5.5: The Good Men of Congo. From left: Fabien, Tuteene, Fred, Joseph, Samuel, Martin

Chapter 6

War, peace and Pamela's Preschool – February 2013

Samuel stops our vehicle metres from the building. An officer in a hammock near the front door casually observes us, but an armed soldier nearby straightens up, his weapon in his hands. I know Samuel is really nervous. But I think about the needs of the children and the expectations of my friends who gave me the money to help build this centre for our Pamela's Preschool. I'm overcome by a righteous anger. How dare this man take over my building! I hop down from the high vehicle as purposefully as my arthritic joints allow and walk towards them. 'Mother,' Samuel warns me 'this is the colonel who threatened to have his soldier shoot me if I took one step in their direction.' I stamp my foot and throw my arms in the air, 'Let him shoot at me if he dares,' I shout, advancing. A voice in my head tells me I'm tempting fate. The officer is getting out of the hammock. He comes to meet me. 'Madam, you seem very upset?' he enquires politely. Perhaps my display has unnerved him? He probably doesn't know what this mad old foreign woman is doing here anyway.

'I am very angry,' I reply, this time faking my anger and hopefully concealing my fear. 'I built this building. It is meant to be a preschool for the children who live here and you have taken it.'

'I am sorry, please do not be disturbed.' He inclines his head. 'In that case, we will move out as soon as possible.'

I can hardly believe my tantrum has been so effective. The colonel indicates that we are free to inspect the not-yet-completed building and Samuel and Tuteene closely follow me. I'm still shaking inside, but as I look around the building it is so much bigger and better than I anticipated from the plans and I can hardly contain my delight. Nevertheless, I can see there is still a lot to be done if the building is to be ready for the official opening ceremony already advertised for 12 February – just five days away.

We get back in our car and drive to Sake. Fabien, and Joseph the builder, are amazed when I tell them the colonel will move out all the ammunition he has stored there, and that the men must get back on the job immediately to have the building ready for the opening. Trying to accomplish as much as possible in the day, we call at the primary and high schools to check on our forty-five sponsored students and then stop off to observe activities at the current site of the preschool class.

After three busy hours we are back at Mubambiro and the Pygmy village. The labourers are idle, sitting by the roadside. As we come to a stop and Samuel asks why they aren't working, we get the bad news. The colonel must have thought I had gone for good – or realised I had no power to evict him. His men have refused them entry and laughed when they protested. 'What can we do now,' I ask Samuel. 'Will we appeal to the District Chief, or the District Police Chief?' He shakes his head, 'They can't challenge the army.' Just then a United Nations helicopter thundered overhead to land nearby on their base. 'But,' Samuel says, his gaze following the helicopter down, 'perhaps we could try the United Nations troops. They are supposed to be here to defend the civilian population.'

It seems our only option. The Blue Bonnets in this area are from Madras, India, and they call themselves the Deccan Devils. They are one group of the nineteen thousand United Nations Mission in the Congo (MONUSCO) forces stationed here to promote 'stabilisation'. I've noticed their vehicles passing up and down the road to their nearby headquarters. At the gate to the high walls around their base I call out to the armed men in the watchtower above: 'I need to speak to your commander.' Might as well go to the top!

A small gate is opened, our vehicle is waved away, and Samuel and I are admitted and ushered into an office. The officer introduces himself; he is not the commander but his adjutant. He listens sympathetically and makes a phone call. The commander apparently has advised him to contact their liaison officer with the Congolese Army stationed in this area. While we wait, we're entertained with cold drinks. Soon, that officer, Major Fidel, arrives. I can see he is outraged when he hears my story. We follow him to the adjacent Congolese military command post for the area, a collection of khaki canvas tents on an open field, and meet the commander. Once more I explain the situation and immediately he is on my side. 'We are fathers, too,' he says. 'Come, we will sort this out.'

The UN Commander joins us. He reminds me of Yul Brynner, the Hollywood actor of *The King and I* fame. Neither man is wearing the insignia of his rank. Samuel explains that this way they are less likely to be targets of snipers. But I think both men are born leaders and their air of command cannot be disguised.

I'm walking between these two powerful men as we approach the disputed building. The colonel is back in his hammock and then he sees us approaching. He tumbles to his feet. 'Oh no!' I think. Although I'm furious with him, I don't want to be just another arrogant colonial lording it over the locals. And even as I think this, my foot slips on the rocky ground, wet in the drizzling rain, and I'm flat on my back. My head hits the ground hard and for a minute I see stars, but then I'm picked up by the two commanders and carried to our vehicle.

I've missed the colonel's encounter with his commander. But as we leave Mubambiro to go back to Goma, the colonel, his hammock and all the explosives and ammunition are out of our building. And the work is under way again at speed.

Figure 6.1: Help from the UN to oust a colonel who had taken over the new preschool building

***

Last September I'd left Goma with the usual emotional goodbyes, though I had no idea what was to happen in the next few months. At that time, the truce with the rebel M23 group seemed to be holding and I had promised to return in six months. This was no longer certain when, within weeks of my departure, the conflict had picked up again. Under the command of several 'generals', the M23 militia had advanced down the highway to attack Goma. The surprised and terrified residents had spent three days cowering in their homes as the mortars rained down on the city, and almost ceaseless gunfire was heard in the streets. Samuel later told me that while many of the doctors and nurses stayed the entire time at the hospital to care for their patients and the wounded, they were short of ambulance drivers. He used his own car to drive around and bring wounded civilians in for treatment.

The gunfire ceased when the Congolese Army was ordered to withdraw and the city was occupied by the M23 on 20 November 2012. The MONUSCO troops, on whose presence everyone had depended, also left the city to the invaders. They were in Congo 'to keep the peace', but they had no mandate to engage in the conflict.

Whether out of fear or a feeling that the invaders might be a better option than the system under which they'd been living, many of Goma's residents supported the M23 troops. The struggle just to feed your family, collect water, burn your rubbish, clothe and educate your children is exhausting for almost everyone in the city. Most people I know just want peace so that they can win their personal ongoing war to survive. The occupying troops were also kept on a tight rein, with no looting or raping permitted, and that rare control would have impressed everyone.

Intrepid members of the international media went into Goma and broadcast film of the city's population demonstrating their support for the victorious M23. But within eleven days, many people must have regretted their public display of rebellion against the government. Reportedly, international pressure on the Ugandan and Rwandan powers thought to be behind the rebels forced them to withdraw to a point six kilometres out of the city. In frustration, as they departed, the M23 looted defenceless civilian homes, their discipline abandoned. Lay preacher Thomson and his family were among those robbed of everything, even the clothes they weren't wearing at the time.

The conflict in Eastern Congo doesn't involve air strikes and there's none of the footage of bombed-out multi-storey buildings that features in televised news reports about other wars around the world. When whole villages of mud and thatch huts are put to the torch, there is little evidence of the destruction left for the cameras. But Mama Virginie told me it was only after the city was taken and the shelling subsided that she realised the iron roof on part of her modest little house had been hit by a mortar round. The family had huddled together in one room for most of the time. The children were crying constantly out of fear and hunger because there was no food for days. Without refrigeration or resources to buy in bulk, families depend on daily shopping for supplies. And it is the informal economy, the daily mini-trade at roadside stalls, that supports the majority of people in the city who don't have regular employment.

Tuteene contacted the Pygmy leaders from Mubambiro, who told him that they'd all fled their homes this time when Sake was taken. They were without shelter or any food aid, just a few hundred among the three million people displaced in the eastern provinces. Most of Fred's relatives fled their homes in Sake and he had twenty people to house and feed in his little two-room shack in Goma. At the time, I approached Rotary International to try to get a delivery of their shelter boxes for homeless people – a wonderfully designed shelter that is easy to construct and is well equipped with essentials for cooking and sleeping. Rotary had a supply across the border in Uganda, but they weren't willing to help: in the past, the inescapable corruption in Congo had meant the boxes often hadn't got to the people in need or had been taken by the rebel militias.

I also got the news that one of the rebel generals made the Bungwe his headquarters during the occupation. He probably slept in what I had come to think of as my bed in Goma! At the same time an American Mennonite missionary was staying there. He had left it too late to escape the city and had come back to the guesthouse, trusting it was the safest place for him (in 2017 this man was on a fact-finding mission for the UN at a site of a massacre in Kasai when he and his female colleague were murdered). It made me think about what I would do if ever I was caught in the city in such a scenario. I have no sense of direction, and although the border with Rwanda isn't far, I couldn't walk there. Nor would I trust one of the men on the motorcycles that substitute for taxis in Goma to take me. I decided that I too would just stay at the Bungwe and hope they could keep me safe.

***

A couple of months later, my friends in Goma began to encourage me to return in February 2013 as I'd planned, even though they said the rebels were still nearby, and I'd heard whispers that not all the M23 leaders had left the city. Incredible as it seemed, on my first day back I'd won the battle with the colonel who had commandeered our building, and we were on track again for the opening ceremony on 12 February. Also, in the process of rescuing our building, I had secured ongoing help for the Pygmies from the Deccan Devils – more like angels in my opinion!

Returning to the village the day after the confrontation with the colonel, I was concerned when I noticed there were so many soldiers everywhere. The houses appeared to be untouched, although the wooden frames of the toilets had been torn down and used for firewood. An officer of the Congolese army had been living in the pigsty, and of course all the pigs as well as the chickens, ducks and goats were gone, eaten by hungry people. When I went to Nyota's house, I panicked because a Bantu woman was there washing a military uniform just outside the door. Maybe the military had taken over the Pygmies' homes too? '*Nyota Wapi?*' (Where is Nyota?), I asked the woman, and she pointed to another area of the village.

I found Nyota near Vumilia's house, where the women were planting cabbage seedlings in a vacant spot. They assured me that the military families were in the village by invitation. 'We know what it is to live like animals. Now we have these beautiful big houses. We invited the soldiers' families to share with us while they are here. Soon they will move on following their men to the next battle front.'

Having heard Nyota's assurances, I still had to wonder if the Pygmies had any choice in this or if their generosity was a good idea: there was such an imbalance of power in the situation and such potential for the Pygmies to be exploited.

Despite the efforts of the women to salvage the kitchen gardens they had planted, nothing much had survived except a few of the banana trees. I had already had the soil evaluated and knew that it was just lava gravel and rocks – the sort of material we would only use as roadfill in Australia. We agreed that a program to improve the soil and the gardening projects should be a priority for the future. Another possibility we discussed in the community meeting was to establish an income-generating project that would benefit everyone. A soap-making project was suggested but Mubawa in particular was advocating for me to fund fishing boats. He argued that the men could then provide the village with fish to eat and the excess of their catch could be sold in Sake market. I didn't know much about commercial fishing and suspected he didn't either. The men admitted that they had sometimes caught fish in the forest by setting dams across a stream and spearing the stranded fish. I was sure fishing on the lake from boats was not that simple. I also knew that none of the men could swim and that the lake was very treacherous. But they introduced a Pygmy man who had been working with a fisherman out of Nsulo and he promised his cooperation in this venture. Mubawa also pointed out that it is quicker and safer to go by boat across the lake than to risk travel on the road in the event of an emergency. A journey by boat is also the best way to get to the nearest public (but not free) hospital, at Kirotshe.

Persuaded by the enthusiasm for fishing boats as well as kitchen gardens, I put both items on the list for funding when I got back to Australia. Fred was commissioned to look into the cost of boats and fishing gear, and a training program for the fishermen, as well as finding a source of fertile soil and determining the cost of trucking it into the village. There are no Flower Power or Bunnings stores in the region to make these projects simple to implement!

***

To everyone's surprise, the new building at Mubambiro progressed enough so that on 12 February we were able to hold the opening ceremony as advertised. It still needed to be painted inside and out, the roof needed lining and we had no furnishings, but it was the most substantial building in the area. Our Deccan Devils provided three marquees, loudspeakers and plastic chairs for the outside ceremony, and the Commander and a squad of his officers attended. The local Traditional Chief, District Chief and the Permanent Secretary for the local Department of Education took part. In the Permanent Secretary's speech, I picked up that at one point he said, 'Only the Australians are helping the Pygmies.' He also said that by law, Pygmies were now to be protected and integrated with local tribes. There are stories from the not-so-distant past of Pygmies being killed and eaten like other 'bush meat', and I had heard there was legislation proposed to ensure an end to this and the blatant discrimination the forest people encountered. But I doubted that there were effective measures in place to enforce it in remote areas.

The whole event was broadcast on local radio as well as on Mishapi Voice, a national TV network. Vumilia, a tiny woman who had only just learnt to read and write in Swahili, spoke confidently into the microphone about what the activities in the centre would mean for the women of the village. Dieudonne, our star student, gave a speech in flawless (they tell me) French. The preschool children did a little dance, and three of the children, all under four years, came up to the microphone to perform little rhymes. The children were all dressed in new uniforms, but since it was a case of one-size-fits-all, a number of the youngest were struggling to keep their skirts or shorts from falling down. The teachers all had matching outfits: long blue-patterned skirts and tops made specially for the occasion. They'd had a similar green outfit made for me. It was far too big, so like the children I was constantly tripping over the skirt, which had to be rolled up and tied around my waist. (That night when I undressed I discovered the green dye had bled out of the material, and it was an effort to scrub it off my skin and out of my underclothes.)

Somewhere in the city, the teachers had bought a bouquet of artificial flowers to present to me, but when little Marie was supposed to hand them to me she wouldn't let go and we had a tug-of-war!

With the speeches over we proceeded to the front door, where I was supposed to cut the ribbon, but at the last moment there were no scissors to be found. Fortunately, Fabien whipped out his trusty scalpel and I managed to slice through the ribbon, then handed the keys to the official from the Department of Education, who handed them to the Traditional Chief who handed them to Mubawa as the Chief of the Pygmies. He had draped himself in palm fronds for the occasion. In lieu of champagne, the education official emptied a bottle of Fanta orange soda over the threshold and everyone crowded into the building for refreshments: the bread rolls and soft drinks I had supplied. I resented the fact that all the dignitaries were served while very few of the Pygmy villagers, much less the children, got even so much as a drink. However, I spread the word that I would be back tomorrow with food supplies. We featured on television from that evening for the next twenty-four hours at every news break!

Figure 6.2: Vumilia making her speech

Figure 6.3: Marie presenting me with flowers

As planned, the building was called 'Pamela's Preschool' in memory of the major donor, Pamela Albany. Sweet-natured and smiling to the end, she had succumbed to motor neurone disease on 28 December 2011.

I had promised to bring food for everyone to celebrate the new building in faith that I would have the money to do so. But first, I had to solve a problem at the bank. Just before the city was taken, I had tried to forward $5000 to meet the expenses for our various programs. After that, all the banks were closed and for a time it seemed as if the transfer had got lost in the emergency. It was with relief the morning after our opening ceremony that Samuel and I found that the funds had finally been credited to our account, giving us the money to spend. The bank manager and half his staff had seen me on the television news the previous night and I was treated like royalty, beginning with a salute from the two guards who sat at the front door with their Kalashnikovs.

Goma city's commercial area is divided into streets which almost exclusively sell a particular item. The streets are narrow, unsealed and congested. People drive according to the rule 'keep going', regardless of whether or not it is possible to see beyond the obstacle in front of you. With some difficulty, Samuel who was also driving, managed to buy sacks of rice, salt and soap powder, and cans of oil. I stayed in the car: it would do nothing for his bargaining power to have a rich foreigner beside him. The poor man must have been exhausted by the time we got to buy the beans, and he parked close to one outlet where he knew the vendor.

I was miles away, mentally planning the remaining activities for the trip, when the vehicle began to rock. A crowd of angry shopkeepers yelling abuse had surrounded the car and were trying to turn it over. I barely had time to think about the danger I was in before Samuel somehow managed to get back in the driver's seat and start the motor. Fortunately, we had some people on our side who were fighting off the people in the front of the vehicle, and we were able to drive away without injuring anyone. Samuel explained that people had lost so much during the occupation of the city that competition for custom was especially cutthroat. He was so tired and we were already so far behind our schedule that he had confined his purchases to one store rather than shopping around to share the business. Those who lost out were venting their disappointment and desperation.

Figure 6.4: Goma street scene

At Mubambiro we now had the building from which to prepare individual sacks and organise an orderly distribution of the supplies. There are sixty-five Pygmy families in the village, but we had enough food to provide a sack for another twenty-one of the poorest refugee families in the area. Even so, I stood at the door with two of the largest of the Pygmy men turning away those hungry people who were not selected. I was glad for once that I couldn't understand their pleas and what I knew must be stories of hardship. When everything was gone and the thankful recipients had made off to enjoy their booty, I noticed that Zaina, the matriarch of the Pygmies, was busy in the deserted building. I thought she was cleaning up, but she was actually salvaging every grain of rice that had fallen to the floor – not one was wasted.

***

While the lake is nearby, the descent to get water is difficult and the water is not safe to drink until treated. Before I left to return home, we installed two 1000-litre tanks at the new centre to gather rainwater, and work began at the back of the building on a large pit-toilet for the children to use. Eucalyptus trees were planted around the building, although it would be some time before they would be big enough to provide shade or a fence. I didn't have much hope for them but we also stuck some bougainvillea cuttings in the barren ground. I ordered fifty multi-coloured mini–plastic chairs and tables for the children and a hundred adult-size chairs for the worship services that would be held on Sundays. On my final day in the country I introduced the teachers to some colourful illustrated storybooks from Australia, including Hans Christian Andersen's story *The Ugly Duckling*. The text was in English but after I told the story, Nsii delighted the children with her version in Swahili. My parting gift was a square of chocolate for everyone.

Figure 6.5: Chocolate treats for the children

Unsure of the security situation, I stayed for just ten days on this trip. I hadn't scheduled any training programs at HAH, but I was included in some special events in the lives of staff members who had become my friends, as well as the chapel services. For example, I was invited to the wedding in Goma of Constance, a supervisor in the psychosocial counselling program. Constance had married a man who on one trip had served as my driver. For this Christian marriage she wore a fabulous white dress with a long train and was accompanied by a dozen attendants, all in white. They processed into the hall to the traditional dance, two steps forward, one step back. The building was packed and I guessed most of the people employed at HAH had been invited. Huge wedding parties seemed to be the norm in Goma and I wondered how people could afford to get married at all. It was clear that most of the 'marriages' among the people at Mubambiro were simple de facto relationships.

I also paid a visit to Clementine, wife of engineer Jean Bizi, shortly after she had given birth to their son, Joshua. It had been a surgical birth, and thinking she needed to rest, I tried to clear the room of all the people who seemed to be partying around her. I discovered that it was the custom for a new mother to be surrounded by well-wishers all day and this would continue for days after the birth!

One day on the way back from Mubambiro I was invited to join members of the hospital staff in a visit to a boy called Amani, whose name means 'peace'. He was a thirteen-year-old orphan from the hospital's Choose Life program for children born HIV positive. His father was dead and his mother had died giving birth to him. He had only an older sister, who at this stage was still well. He had been an inpatient at the hospital for years but had now gone home to die in his native village at Nsulo. This village is located high on a hillside above Lake Kivu and a camp for displaced people. I struggled up the steep incline with one hand on Samuel's shoulder while engineer Bizi had a hand on my back propelling me forward.

Samuel told me Amani had asked to be baptised in the pool at the hospital chapel before returning to his village. The staff had feared the immersion would kill him and when I saw his emaciated body and the raw sores all over him I could understand why. He lay on the floor in a poor hut where the cold wind off the lake swept through the cracks in the walls. The visitors gathered around, prayed and sang hymns. Amani's eyes rolled back in his head from time to time, but he reached out and took my hand as I bent to give him my love and blessing as we left. One of the hospital's community nurses stayed with him and his sister. When we were on the outskirts of Goma about half an hour later, she telephoned Samuel to say Amani had peacefully breathed his last.

Figure 6.6: Saying goodbye to Amani

I had to be thankful Amani was out of his suffering, but shed a few tears as we fought the peak-hour traffic into the city on yet another narrow and rough detour. It was most annoying that someone kept sounding their horn when it was quite obvious there was no way anyone could hurry up or allow anyone to pass. The sound was deafening and I turned around to glare at the people in the vehicle behind us. Suddenly, engineer Bizi, who was driving, stopped the car and hopped out. I wondered what on earth had come over him. He went to the front of our vehicle, lifted the bonnet and suddenly there was quiet. It was our horn which had become stuck! We laughed hysterically all the way into the city, releasing the pent-up emotions from the scene at the deathbed of that poor child.

I departed Congo the next day. There was a serendipitous meeting on the plane from Kigali to Johannesburg with the British Ambassador to Rwanda and Burundi, and his family. He told me that given Australia had no diplomats in Congo, during the increased conflict a few months ago he had been involved in getting an Australian biologist studying butterflies safely out of the Congolese forests. He kindly gave me his contact details for future reference. A reassuring encounter as I plan my next trip for September.

Chapter 7

Rockdale – September 2013

'This visit is all about establishing activities to promote self-sufficiency for the villagers', I explain to Alexandra, a freelance journalist who has come to make a film about the village (subsequently aired on ABC program *Lateline* on 11 April 2014). 'The chief men in the village have asked for a fishing project and funds have been donated by the Rotary Club of Rockdale City to build and equip two fishing boats.' Escorted by an excited crowd of Pygmy men, I lead her around the back of Pamela's Preschool to the place where the two boats have been built. One has been painted a bright blue and on the side the name *Rockdale* stands out in white. I laugh. 'That will please my friends at the Rotary Club.' Nearby, Nsii is hanging on to a wayward goat, who maybe senses this won't be a good day for him. I pat his silky, coal-black coat, apologising for what is to happen to him, and he wags his little tail like a dog. 'Has he had a good last meal as I requested?' I ask Mubawa, who has been most anxious to see this project get under way. He nods, but I doubt this is the case.

Alex focuses her camera on the action as the MONUSCO troops arrive with their truck and help the cheering Pygmy men load the blue boat onto their vehicle. Then the UN helpers drive off, their truck loaded with the boat, the men who loaded the boat, the Bantu fishermen I've hired to teach the Pygmies to fish on the lake, the proud Pygmies chosen to be the fishermen for their village, and Alex and the goat. The rest of us hasten down to the MONUSCO jetty on foot, having been granted rare access to their land. The road down to the foreshore within their base is the only place where we could get our boats down the steep, rocky incline to the foreshore and onto the lake. I thank the troops from India without whose help this would have been impossible. The unit that helped us last year has returned home to India but the new troops and their leaders are equally helpful. This commander is a wise man who has set up a small animal farm on the base, mostly rabbits, not to eat, but for his men to care for. He explains that caring for the rabbits relieves the boredom when the men are off-duty and offers them an outlet for affection while they are so far from the people they love. While we wait for the vehicle with the boat to arrive, he arranges for Samuel and me to be served delicious little vegetarian samosas.

Once they arrive at the jetty, the Pygmy sailors don life-jackets under instruction from the local fishermen and board the boat for the first time, along with the goat and Alex. At last the blue boat is pushed out onto the waters of the lake and Samuel holds up his hand to bless the launch. I breathe a sigh of relief when it doesn't sink – especially because I feel a degree of responsibility for Alex. Once the boat is free of the shallows, Mumbere, one of the professional fishermen, casts out the fishing net in one graceful movement. It is a serenely beautiful scene with the misty mountains in the background, the blue waters of the lake and a green headland in front of us. I note the nets: I had to pay for them to be made, there being no fishing equipment stores where such tools of the trade could be purchased off the shelf. I couldn't understand why there had to be two sets of nets – one for large fish and one for the small species. It seemed to me that closely woven nets for small fish would be just as appropriate for the large fish. But I lost that argument.

For a while we crowd at the lakeside in the UN compound watching the boat's progress, but we must now make it back to the rocky foreshore nearest the village where the boats will moor. I make slow progress carefully clambering down through the jumble of jagged boulders to the water's edge, hoping not to sprain an ankle or break a leg but eager to be in the midst of all the ceremonies. Unfortunately, I arrive in time to see Mubawa inexpertly slit the goat's throat and collect the bright red blood to anoint the prow of the boat. Alex puts the camera in front of me for a comment on this traditional sacrifice. What could I say? It's the custom and only having done so will the men feel it is safe to take the boat out. Lake Kivu is the second deepest lake in the world. I've heard stories of a female monster who drags people to their death in its depths. Most likely the people get caught up on submerged objects or overcome by pockets of methane gas which rise to the surface every so often. Tragically, this was probably the fate of one of those young Australian Congolese who had gone for a swim with me in the buoyant salt waters of the baths on the shores of Botany Bay in 2012, only a year before his death. He'd returned to Congo and on his first day back, perhaps because he was overconfident of his skill, drowned when he went for a swim in the unfamiliar depths of the cold, fresh waters of Lake Kivu.

Back at the village in the preschool yard, the women have lit charcoal fires to prepare a feast of *fufu* (a cassava flour mix) and goat stew in the huge cooking pots used to prepare the meals for the children. While bush meats, such as small deer, rabbits and even monkeys, were a prized part of the diet in the forest, now meat of any kind is rarely on the menu for people in this area and the unmistakable aroma of the cooking brings envious passers-by to investigate. I don't know why I'm surprised when only the men go into the building and sit down to gorge themselves. After about half an hour of feasting, it seems they have had their fill and Mubawa comes out and rounds up any little boys in sight and takes them in for the leftovers. When the barest of bones are left, the women who have laboured over the hot fires go in and clean up.

Figure 7.1: Launching the fishing boat called Rockdale

Figure 7.2: Preparing fufu for the feast for men only

At least I was satisfied that all the children under six years old, boys and girls, were eating every day at the preschool. Most days it would be cabbage and sweet potato with rice or beans on alternate days. On my last visit I'd left instructions to enrol not more than thirty-five children, but later agreed to accept fifteen more children from the local tribe. However, when I arrived at the preschool the day after the boat launch, there were seventy children present. I tried to explain that that number of children was far too many for the three teachers to manage. But Nsii protested that the military brought their children to her and she couldn't argue with a man with a gun. It was chaos as the teachers tried to wash seventy pairs of grubby little hands in a single plastic basin without running water, cook the food on charcoal fires, then serve the meals and help feed the youngest children. All this was caught on camera by Alex. I suggested that the teachers organise for the children to eat in relays. The idea was met with horror. The children must all eat at the same time!

Many people in Australia want to give me clothes and toys for the children, but there's no post into Goma and only so much I can carry in my luggage. Money is more useful and allows me to buy appropriate items in Goma and so stimulate the local economy. However, since 2009 the incredibly generous owner of a huge pathology company in Sydney, Sonic Healthcare – Douglass Hanly Moir Pathology, has been sending a container up to twice a year to HAH. Over the years, Sonic has built and equipped an excellent pathology department at HAH, sent experts to train staff to use and maintain the sophisticated machines in the laboratory, and funded a local doctor to become Eastern Congo's only pathologist. I was able to send some items in one of these containers, which came via sea to the Tanzanian coast then overland through Tanzania and Rwanda and into Goma. It had recently arrived in Goma and been unloaded, so I was able to bring the toys and games donated in Australia out to the village myself. The children took turns on the xylophones, tambourines and clappers to bang and shake with all their might. Every child received a new shirt and a skirt or shorts from a Sydney junior tennis school, and there were enough recycled Qantas blankets from Overseas Disaster Services in Sydney for every family to have one.

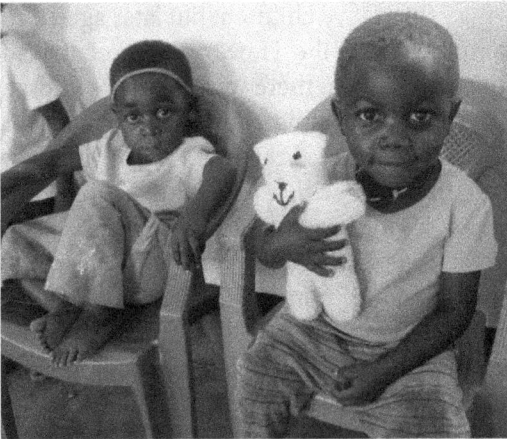

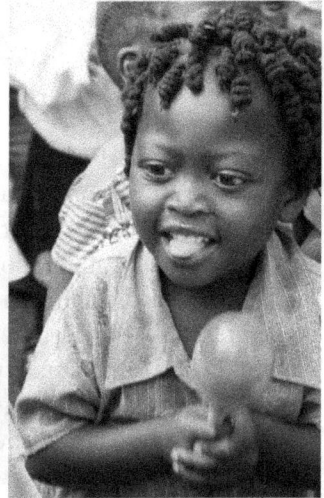

Figure 7.3 and 7.4: Toys from donors in Australia were appreciated by the children, although parents would have preferred cash to buy food

Figure 7.5: Preschool graduates celebrating being chosen to go on to primary school

Nsii told me that twenty-five of the preschool children had turned six and should be graduating to primary school. We were already paying fees for fifty children at primary and high schools and I consulted their examination results to help me decide which children to continue to sponsor. As difficult as these decisions were, I could only enrol children who were coping with the lessons, especially when there were younger, potentially bright children coming from the preschool who deserved the opportunity to go on to primary classes. Every child in primary school had passed this year and it occurred to me that the principal had realised that this was how I chose the children to sponsor. I ended up paying for a total of sixty children. That meant sixty children whose parents could not provide for them to eat every day would have a daily meal courtesy of the World Food Program.

Evelyn's literacy classes three afternoons each week for a dozen of the men and women in the village were a great success. Especially impressive was the way she integrated ideas about basic human rights into her lessons. Even if just a handful of the adults in the village are able to read and write and understand that they have rights there will be less chance of anyone being exploited as they have been in the past.

Figure 7.6: Evelyn's literacy class

I'd heard that Evelyn had been raped as a teenager but only now was there time for us to sit together in private in our building for me to hear her life story. Although her father was not a Pygmy she had grown up with her mother's people, but her father had taken enough interest in her to pay for her to go to school. About ten years ago when she was sixteen, she and two other Pygmy girls were gathering firewood at the edge of the forest when they were surprised by soldiers. They dragged the terrified girls far into the forest and gave them the option of dying or submitting to rape. Evelyn thought, 'Why should I die like so many others?' even while knowing that by complying she would be branded a slut by most people. All of the girls submitted to the rape but afterwards one of the men wanted to kill them anyway. Another man persuaded the group to let them live, but they took knives, cut off one girl's breast, and slashed the second girl's arms to the bone. A knife was held to Evelyn's neck and she thought he intended to slit her throat. Instead, he made a cut from behind her head, down and around her throat. I have heard that some rebel militias choose a specific way of mutilating women so that they can be identified as victims of that particular group. Their commanders actually encourage this brutality because it gives them notoriety, and notoriety can ensure a place of influence at peace talks.

Evelyn knew she was lucky to have survived when one of the girls died of her wounds, but several months later she realised she was pregnant. At the time, she never imagined that her subsequent treatment at HAH and the literacy training she received at The City of Joy (a rehabilitation centre for rape survivors) in South Kivu would give her the opportunity for a better life than most of her friends. The child she bore fortunately looks like her, but she said she would have kept him anyway. For some women, the child born of rape is not only a constant reminder of the rapist but also makes both of them outcasts. I visited one orphanage where there were two thousand children and many were the children of rape. One of the infants I met there had a wound in his side from the bullet which killed his mother when he was still in her womb.

I asked Evelyn if any of the Pygmy women in the village had been raped. She counted up fifteen women that she knew of, adding that others would undoubtedly have kept it secret. This is a problem for Pygmy and Bantu women alike, especially for unmarried girls if they become pregnant as a consequence. If they have come forward within seventy-two hours of the rape they can have the 'morning after' pill. But if they don't declare what has happened until their pregnancy is obvious, no one will believe their story and they will be considered prostitutes. Worse yet for rape survivors, the militia are all too often infected with HIV. When a woman conceals her rape, whether out of shame, fear of being rejected by her husband, or even because rape is so prevalent that she accepts it as normal, then the possibility of infecting other family members increases. Two other factors compound the problem in Pygmy bands: the lack of information about their rights so that they rarely think it is worth reporting their assault, and their traditional practice of engaging in sexual activity at a young age and marrying before they're eighteen years old.

Evelyn had also informally adopted a niece and nephew, children of one of her brothers, a soldier who had been missing, presumed dead, for eight years. The dead are not always counted nor bodies retrieved after military action in remote areas, and many wives are left in limbo. Evelyn's sister-in-law wanted to make a new life unencumbered by her children, and Evelyn had raised them as her own. Evelyn's story is widely known and she told me she was happy to share these details to make people aware of the difficulties rape survivors encounter, and so help women who face a similar situation.

***

Every year I recognised deficits in the village project, which had developed in response to needs as they were presented to me rather than as a carefully planned development scheme. The lack of accurate data on the residents in the village was part of the problem. We only had a list of heads of the sixty-five households that Fred had made when the village was planned. There hadn't been a census in Congo since 1986, and in any case Pygmies were unlikely to have been registered, so there were no official statistics to draw on. Always ready to take on extra duties, this year Evelyn compiled a very useful and comprehensive survey of the village residents, including the ages of the children so that for the future I had some data for planning school admissions. There were some surprises in the survey. The two leading men each had three houses for their three wives and their children. Officially in the village there were forty-three women, twenty-nine of whom were widows, thirty men and 120 children under fifteen years of age. But, as Evelyn explained, the numbers in each house varied from week to week as relatives came and went, and as people died and women gave birth. And adding to the congestion in the village, thirty families from the group I visited in Kitshanga had taken refuge here, camped around the houses.

Between my visits to Congo, the Good Men had kept me up to date on the progress of the sewing and garden projects in the village. In 2010, I had tried to organise for five women to learn to be tailors. However, the classes were held in Sake and it was too far for the women to walk there and back every day and still find time for essential activities such as getting water, searching for firewood and begging for scraps of food. Now that we had a building within the village and could store equipment safely, I'd hired a local tailor to hold classes three afternoons a week after the preschool children had gone home. Twenty women signed up for the classes, including Giselle, now a pretty and healthy young woman, and I paid for three hand machines, tables and one treadle machine, as well as cloth and cottons, tape measures and scissors.

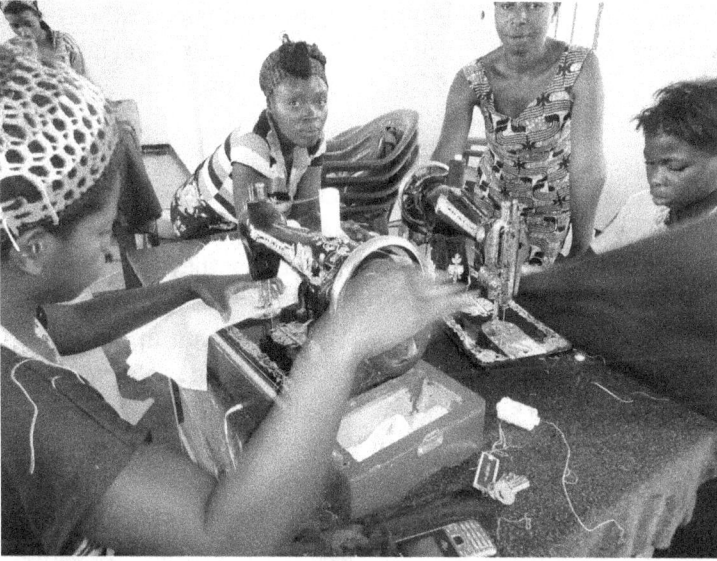

Figure 7.7: Women participating
in a sewing class

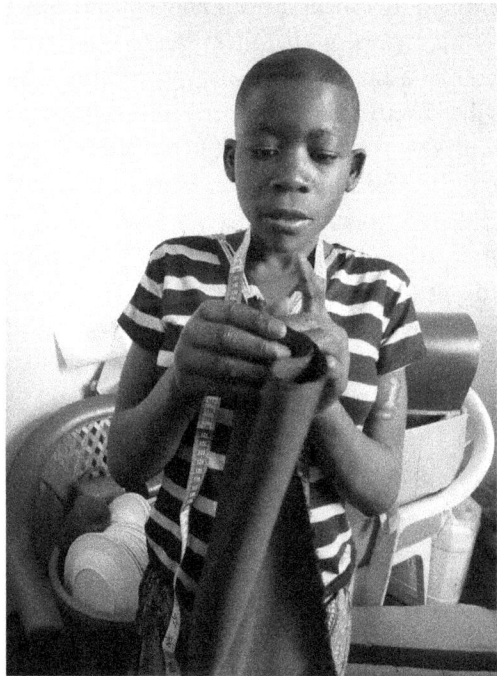

Figure 7.8: Giselle learning to use a
tape measure and scissors

The women had made good progress in using the machines and were well on the way to being able to set up their own small businesses and hopefully able to make the school uniforms for the village children, and also to sell their wares in the nearby market at Sake. But one day I noticed that only Wamini, the teacher, was cutting the material for the women to sew. She explained that none of the women had ever used a pair of scissors before and she feared they would ruin too much material learning this skill. We quickly found scraps that they could practise on so that they would have all the essential skills.

A few months ago I'd attended a workshop on setting up raised-bed gardens organised by my local council at Rockdale in Sydney and realised it was the best way to establish kitchen gardens in this infertile area. Someone suggested that the Pygmy village with its rocky grounds could also be called Rockdale, but the ready availability of rocks to construct the perimeters of the raised beds was an asset in this project. The local Ministry of Agriculture gave permission for us to truck in fertile soil for the gardens, and Samuel introduced an agronomist called Wilfreda to work in the village. She had trained in Tanzania with an Australian-funded program and already done similar work with other Pygmy groups, so she knew how to win their cooperation. By the time I met her she had already been working in the village setting up seed beds for cabbages, tomatoes and leeks and working with the preschool children to establish a demonstration garden where the children had planted and were looking after a thriving crop of cabbages. I agreed to continue paying Wilfreda to spend several days in the village each week helping to set up the gardens for every family and teaching the principles of recycling and permaculture. Trucking in good soil was expensive but essential to the success of the project. The total quote per family to set up these gardens for the sixty-five homes in the village was US$150.

Figure 7.9: Vumilia's raised-bed kitchen garden

Figure 7.10: The children tend the preschool cabbage patch

The gardens of course needed water in the dry season, and it was hard work for the women and young girls to struggle up and down the rocky foreshore to the lake with the heavy yellow jerry cans. For the gardens especially, but also for general use, we installed additional pipes and two new faucets at strategic places in the village to connect to the major pipeline from the lake, which had been put in by MONUSCO engineers. One of our neighbours declared that the major pipeline was his, and demanded that the Pygmies pay rent for the use of the water. This would have worked if the Good Men had not stepped in to protect them. But this was just one of the problems the Pygmies had with their neighbours. A man who had recently bought land adjoining the Pygmy village told them a whole section, including a row of houses, was actually his property. Maitre Martin had to come to the village with his friend from the Lands Office to put this man in no doubt about the actual boundaries of Pygmy land.

Another issue with neighbours arose over the water tanks we'd installed to provide safe drinking water for the children in the preschool. Access to safe drinking water was a problem for everyone in the area. A stream ran behind the village down to the lake, but the water was polluted by the many uses upstream, especially drivers stopping their trucks on the side of the road to wash off the mud from long-distance hauls. Unfortunately, all runoff water in this region contains high levels of minerals found in the volcanic rocks, and drinking this water tends to discolour teeth. At first I'd assumed that everyone I met had serious tooth decay.

Once the military families in the camp near the village had seen our tanks, they'd come and used the water to wash themselves, their uniforms and household items. The tanks had quickly been emptied and the surrounds had become a quagmire of waste water. The Good Men tried to stop this by putting locks on the taps, only to find the taps broken and the tanks empty again the next day. Now the tanks would have to stay dry until the next rains came in November, but we repaired the taps in the hope that people would be content to use the new pipes and faucets we'd installed in the village rather than the tank water at the preschool. After considering all these issues I decided to build a high stone fence around the perimeter of our centre to ensure the security of the main building and its contents, and the toilets, shed and water tanks.

However, the problems with neighbours and military coming into the village were more difficult to control and sometimes were of the Pygmies' own making. Last year some of the Pygmy women had taken pity on the military families and invited them to share their homes, but subsequently some of the more enterprising families had started charging their guests rent. A good idea at first glance, but I'd always feared it might eventually be difficult for them to get their boarders out if they made trouble. In fact, there was already a problem associated with their presence. For example, one soldier's wife had set up a stall to sell alcohol and cigarettes, and her husband and his mates had taken over this section of the village, sometimes preventing Pygmies from passing through on the way to their homes.

Foolishly, I went to see the situation for myself and came upon a group of uniformed men blocking access to a row of houses. I was met with hostile glares and comments which it was probably just as well I didn't understand. The men obviously had drunk too much alcohol, so I beat a hasty retreat. I reported the problem to the MONUSCO friends, and the adjutant came back to the village with me to investigate. But someone must have warned the soldiers because they'd left the area by the time we got back, or so I thought. The adjutant suggested that if there was any more trouble Alex should take photos as evidence. Almost immediately after he left us the group of soldiers were back, more noisy and belligerent than ever. Alex raised her camera to capture their behaviour on film – a dangerous move! One of the soldiers was so drunk by now he had no inhibitions and charged her, reaching for the camera, and swiping at Alex's head. Fortunately, his mates realised that was going too far and pulled him away.

We took the film of the incident to the adjutant and I heard that as a result, the man was identified and disciplined. It's painful to think what that meant. I had to pity the men in Congo. Many of those who joined either the regular army or the militias had little choice in what they did with their lives. The lower ranks in any of the armies were recruited from families living in absolute poverty with the promise of a uniform and meals. Their officers, I was told, might be delinquent young men from affluent families, banished to the military as a last chance to reform.

Then there were the child soldiers, at one time numbering thirty thousand. In 2009, I'd heard that there were still around eight thousand, some of whom were girls. The children were abducted from their homes and forced to commit atrocities that made them afraid to try to escape back to their families. The girls were forced into sexual slavery as well as working as porters of supplies, arms and ammunition when the militia were on the move. One teenage girl who managed to escape reported that she was pregnant, which almost guaranteed she would be shot. Everyone involved as a combatant in the ongoing low-level war in the east of Congo lived in miserable circumstances with early death a strong possibility.

***

The funds donated by my friends and family for the people at Mubambiro had no strings attached. No one was coerced into attending the Christian services Thomson from the Katindo Anglican Church in Goma had been conducting in our building. During the war in Vietnam I'd seen the problem of aid being associated with profession of faith when people joined churches just to get material benefits; 'rice Christians' they were called. But every Sunday Thomson filled the building with Pygmies, military wives and displaced people. He'd set up a Sunday school class for the children and brought women from the Anglican Church in Goma to help the Pygmy women set up their own Mothers Union, which aimed for women to support one another in family crises. He'd held meetings where people rejected the witch doctor and burnt their charms and amulets, and he'd conducted multiple baptisms in the stream that formed a border at the back of the village – mostly in the wet season when the water was running reasonably clear.

When I'd arrived in Goma this trip, Thomson had told me that twenty-three people were now ready to be confirmed into the Anglican Church and the bishop was coming from his diocesan headquarters at Bukavu in South Kivu to perform the ceremony on one of the Sundays I'd be in Congo. There'd been some debate about where the service was to be held, but Thomson said the Pygmies insisted it had to be in their 'church' at Mubambiro while I was there to attend or they wouldn't participate at all.

Bishop Bahati wasn't a young man and was probably exhausted by the time he'd made the overnight lake crossing by ferry from Bukavu to Goma and then travelled more than an hour on the bumpy road to Mubambiro. The building was packed; the Pygmy choir danced and sang to the beat of drums. The bishop, in brocade robes, mitred hat, his ornate shepherd's crook in hand, processed in with an entourage of four other white-robed clergy. In his address, he did mention that he'd had some trepidation about coming for the first time to this area, knowing that a rebel army was camped barely a few kilometres away. He sat on a makeshift throne to bless the seventy confirmees in groups of three, Pygmy and Bantu kneeling together, one in their profession of faith.

As I left the village for the last time this trip I was farewelled as usual by a large number of people. One small boy led us in the procession to the car, holding aloft a long stick which he had shaped at the top in imitation of the bishop's crook.

Figure 7.11: A baptism in the stream at the end of the village

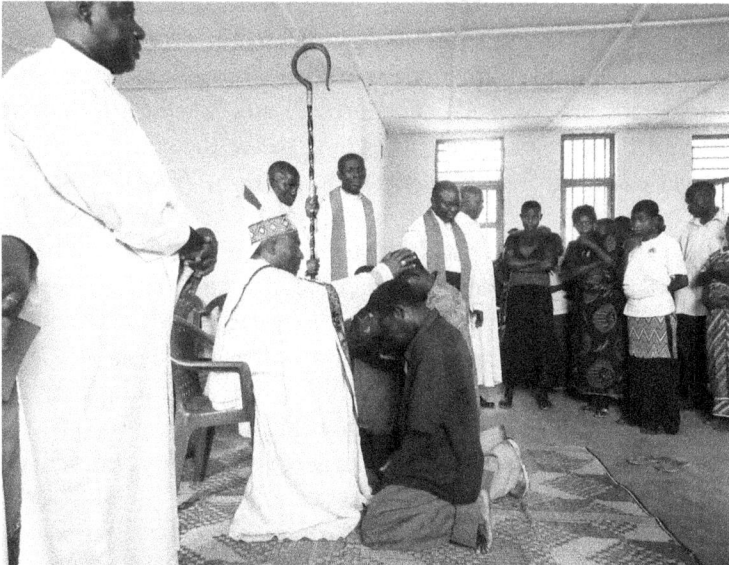

Figure 7.12: Anglican Bishop Bahati confirming Pygmy and Bantu one in their faith

Chapter 8

Into the forest – September 2014

'We enter the forest here.' Jules, the ranger, points to a wire fence. I reach for the wire to lift it and get through. Akura grabs my hand before I can touch it and I realise it's electrified to keep wild animals in and domestic animals out.

I'm already a little breathless and tired. This morning I got up and had a quick breakfast for a 5 a.m. departure from the guesthouse. As Samuel and I left Goma city behind, the sky was lightening behind three indigo-dark volcanoes. Intermittently, pure white puffs of smoke popped from the summit of one. Since then it has been a rough two-hour drive on a narrow road, climbing the mountain all the way, and just now, thirty minutes of hiking over rocky ground. It wouldn't be so bad if we weren't wearing heavy clothing. The black mackintosh, the only heavy wet-weather gear available in Goma, is already weighing me down. I'm also wearing three layers of clothes in anticipation of cold, wet weather in the depths of the forest.

'We must crawl under the wire,' Jules advises. I'm determined to go through with this, having come so far. I fall to the ground, the only way I know to get there given my knee problems. Some women have come to work in nearby tobacco fields and they call out, laughter in their voices, 'Is the *mzungu mzee* (old foreigner) going to see the gorillas?' I'm as low as I can get on the ground but lift my head to say, '*Ndiyo!* (Yes!)' They're laughing outright now and I roll myself under the wire, expecting any moment to feel an electric shock. Instead, I've landed in a bed of nettles. The layers of clothes I'm wearing have protected most of me, except for my face and hands. I can't get up so the men hoist me to my feet. Akura wields his machete on some nearby bamboo and presents me with a walking stick. It is hardly thicker than my thumb but I lean on it and find it takes my full weight, barely bending at all. Akura goes ahead, cutting a path with his machete and already we seem to be in dense forest. Almost immediately he is disappearing into the foliage of the trees and I force myself to pick up the pace. Samuel, and Jules with his rifle, are behind me, but I think Akura is the safest one to be with.

My legs are turning to jelly. I've been struggling on, keeping glimpses of Akura's blue shirt in sight for over an hour, and I've fallen over at least three times. The strange thing is that I fall over backwards and land on my behind. Jules picks me up once more and then points at some marks in the mud ahead, 'Look! Elephant tracks!' he says excitedly. Samuel plunges ahead of me to keep up with Akura, while I wonder how on earth an elephant could get through this tangle of trees and the thick undergrowth of plants. I keep hitting my forehead on low-hanging branches that are covered in moss. Akura now turns around to indicate more animal tracks – wild buffalo or deer?

Another hour and I can hardly walk; my legs are like lead now and my breath laboured. I think I'm going to pass out, and gagging, start to retch. Jules and Akura are anxious that not even a drop of my gastric juices should fall to the forest floor, but I have no control over what is happening. I sink to the ground and they clear a space and help me to sit more comfortably. I feel so bad I wonder if I will die here. I look up and can barely see a patch of sky through the canopy and think that even if there was a rescue helicopter the crew couldn't find me down here. Almost as if he reads my mind, Jules assures me if I can't continue they will carry me back to the base. He adds that they did that for a woman working with the UN who came here just a few weeks ago and collapsed. It's probably altitude sickness.

After they help me take off the heavy raingear and a layer of the warm clothes I feel a little better, though I am wet to the skin. Samuel puts his hands on my shoulders as if to give me his strength, saying, 'You are OK, my mother, nothing bad is happening to you.' I feel the nausea lifting and find the strength to stand up. I ask if they think we might meet the gorillas soon and Samuel encourages me, 'Not too far now.' But Akura shakes his head so I wonder if Samuel just doesn't want me to give up. Nevertheless, I begin to experience the forest in a new way. The air is damp but it isn't raining. The leaves ruffle and rustle in a slight breeze and I'm conscious of the constant hum of countless insects, but apart from that there is a benign stillness that calms and reassures me. I think about my Pygmy friends' belief that the Forest is also a manifestation of the Eternal Divine Creator and I walk on in a completely different frame of mind.

I've visited the forest this trip partly because the Congolese Government has approved oil exploration in this wilderness and national treasure, Virunga National Forest; I want to see it before it is despoiled. But I also want to see how the Pygmies lived prior to their expulsion from their traditional home. The women told me it was a difficult life – their only good memory was of the season when the wild honey was ready to be harvested. The older men were more positive. When they talked about hunting, their excitement and pride rekindled. I'm beginning to understand their nostalgia for their former way of life and really admire them for their survival skills, none of which are relevant now in the village at Mubambiro. Seseti, the patriarch, once fixed his eyes on mine and said, 'Please ask the government to give us back our mountain for it is ours and we want it back.' But I doubt if any of the generation born out of the forest could live here now, or would want to.

We're coming through a stand of bamboo which has been devastated, all the vegetation stripped and trampled down. Akura turns to beam at me. 'The gorillas were feasting here quite recently, we are very near now.' At last from somewhere nearby I hear a low-pitched growl. Jules holds up his hand for us to stop and answers with a high-pitched rise and fall of his voice. The gorilla answers in a single grunt, obviously no longer alarmed. 'He knows me,' Jules says.

We stop the required seven metres from a giant silverback. 'This is Humba, he weighs 220 kilograms and must eat 30 kilograms of vegetation every day to survive. He has a small family of two females, an adult son and two babies.' Here come the fluffy black babies cavorting over their father, who was having a little nap, swinging on vines and tumbling through the undergrowth towards us. They pound their chests and Jules explains that this is a greeting and not a sign of aggression. But, 'Do not touch his babies,' Jules warns, 'If he comes near, you must crouch down, never turn your back and never run away from him.' Humba decides to follow his babies. I could put out my hand and touch him. 'Are you afraid,' Jules whispers. 'Never!' Rather, I'm thrilled by the experience of being so close to this superb wild creature in his own environment.

He isn't interested in us, only in finding the juiciest bamboo shoots. With one powerful arm, he reaches up to grasp a stem almost as thick as a tree trunk and it comes crashing down on us. We stifle our startled laughter and he looks at us for a moment before continuing his meal, peeling back the outer husk with fingers that look so human. He shrugs off the insects that, thankfully, stick to him rather than bothering me. In no time at all he has demolished that bamboo stem and begins to pull down another. He stops even as he is about to exert the effort to break the stem, looks full at us and deliberately pulls it in the other direction so that it doesn't land on us again. I have known and dearly loved a number of cats, a German shepherd dog and some surprisingly intelligent birds in my life, but I think this experience of another species' understanding, even compassion, is extraordinary and immensely precious.

Figure 8.1: Venturing into the forest

We stay an hour with the family until they've made the most of the bamboo in this stand and the giant silverback lumbers off with the family following. I get up with difficulty and mixed relief and sadness. We start to retrace our steps on the same trail Akura hacked for us to get here. Only now I realise why I kept falling backwards – it is a steep incline and now the challenge for me is not to fall forward onto my face. I remind the men that I am an old woman of seventy-five years with arthritic knees, but even so we're making better time getting down the mountain. I'm glad it hasn't rained, which would have made the track dangerously slippery.

After more than an hour the men are joking about something. Samuel says that we are near the place where I almost passed out. Suddenly, Akura is shouting and Jules shoots past me; Samuel, too. I am about to protest but suddenly I understand he has yelled, 'Fire ants!' I can see a swarm of them across the track and all over my thick boots and almost immediately feel them at my neck and running down inside my collar. 'They're biting me,' I scream. 'They are biting us, too!' Samuel screams back. I keep going, telling myself I must not fall over, they will be in my ears and nose and mouth in moments. I know they can kill small animals.

It is a relief to see Akura has at last come to the section of electrified fence where we entered the forest. I don't hesitate but am down, under and up, and like the men, tearing off my clothes to get at the ants in my underwear. The women who were starting work in the fields when we went into the forest almost six hours ago are preparing to leave. They call out, 'Did the *mzungu mzee* see the gorillas?' '*Ndiyo!*' I yell back, and am rewarded with a burst of triumphant African ululation. Samuel turns to me, 'You have done what women much younger than you cannot do.' 'But,' he adds, 'terrible experience!'

Even once we're out of the forest we have a half-hour hike and two hours' drive ahead of us before we can get clean, eat and rest. At last in the car, we're forced to make a detour because of landmines on the more direct route. Slowly descending the steep and slippery road down the mountain in a light rain, Samuel tells me that the ants were attracted by my spilled gastric juices, and that he was very afraid we would meet elephants – or even the deadly mambo snake. A thought that, mercifully, hadn't even occurred to me when we were in the forest.

That night when I put my muddy socks in the sink to wash them, countless dead ants float out. Another mercy, I decide, since they'd died in the dense weave of the wool before they could bite me!

***

The visit to the forest was a welcome interlude after a big disappointment when I arrived here this trip. The fishing project had failed altogether. I felt frustrated because I was always doubtful about this enterprise, but Mubawa and Alexis had assured me they would see it through. It was a project that was wanted and needed, but the capacity wasn't there. First, they were not prepared for the hard work involved: the cold nights on the lake, and the uncertain success. Local fishermen know where to cast the nets and even they do not always get a good catch. The surplus of food the men had expected just never happened. And within weeks of my departure, one of the Pygmy men from the village decided he could take the larger of the boats out by himself. He wasn't wearing a life-jacket, although the necessity for that had been emphasised over and over again. From the shore, the other men shouted a challenge. He stood up to respond and fell overboard. No one could swim, and at first they thought he was playing a joke on them, so no one tried to rescue him. It took the MONUSCO sailors four days to recover his body. His name was Safari Sasa, meaning 'good journey', but his last journey certainly wasn't good.

The boat from which Sasa fell had not been blessed at first launch and so now was considered cursed. No one wanted to get in it so I had approved its sale. Alexis had bought chickens, ducks and goats with the proceeds and distributed them throughout the village to all the families, but the price he said he got for the boat was far less than the money I'd invested in its construction. Particularly distressing was that someone had to take the blame for Sasa's death. The authorities fixed on Mumbere, the local fisherman I'd hired to teach the Pygmies. Unbeknown to me until I got back here, he'd been in prison for three months. During that time, without his support for the family, one of his small sons had died. Fred, who was supposed to be monitoring this project, disappeared soon after the incident. Now I understood why I hadn't heard from him for months.

As if this wasn't bad enough, the blue boat called *Rockdale* had been confiscated by the new MONUSCO troops stationed at Mubambiro. Our Indian angels had been replaced by men from South Africa. I expected that they would happily release the boat to me, since I'd paid for it and could identify it. I certainly didn't think there would be another blue boat called *Rockdale* anywhere in Congo. Samuel and I went to their base to get it back, but when we met with a group of stern-faced South African officers they explained why they'd taken the boat. First, a member of the village had made an arrangement with some of the MONUSCO troops to use the boat to ferry prostitutes across to them at night. But worse, the officers were sure that over a few months one of the Pygmy men had stolen many cans of diesel oil from their stores, using the boat to get into their warehouse on the lake shores. When he was almost caught in the act, he dived overboard, abandoning the boat, and swam away. All of the Pygmy men denied they'd been involved, and I made the point that even if it was someone from the Pygmy village, he must have had insider help from the South Africans – but of course that didn't exonerate him.

The senior South African officer indicated that someone had to take responsibility for the theft. I stared at him, wondering what this meant: did they want me to pay for the stolen diesel oil, or go to prison? The officer went on to say that since I'd been far away in Australia it was Samuel, my representative and assistant, who was responsible for supervising the actions of the Pygmies. I started to defend him, but the South African politely told me to stay out of it, and Samuel, trembling from head to foot, humbly took responsibility and apologised profusely. Nothing was said about anyone going to prison and I made a deal with them to get the boat back. I could see the fishing project was doomed and decided that we should give the boat to poor Mumbere as compensation for his time in prison. Alexis and Mubawa, as representatives of the villagers, agreed to this arrangement, and they put their mark on a document relinquishing all claim to the boat in the future.

This wasn't quite the end of the fishing debacle. The dead man's family came to me demanding I pay them compensation. Most vocal was his sister and her husband, who had never been part of the original villagers. In the background, I recognised Nyantu, his shy little widow with her three young children. When I had a chance to speak with her privately, I discovered that her sister-in-law had evicted her and the children from their home. They were once again destitute and sleeping in the open. I already knew that customarily a dead man's property belongs to his birth family, not his wife and children. But since Sasa's sister was not listed on the deeds for the land she had no legal right to live in the village in any case, and we were able to return the house to Nyantu and her children. I gave her cash to replace the possessions that had been removed. I'm not sure how long we will need to monitor this situation but for now the little family were back in their home and their oldest child was back in school.

***

For the new school year I'd enrolled forty-five children in the local primary school and five in the high school. Dieudonne had met expectations and passed the State Finals Examinations at his first attempt. All along he'd said he wanted to go to university to study to be an engineer. I was ambivalent about promising to help because the fees at what is called the 'free' university in Goma are very high and then there were all the living expenses I would have to meet since he had no family support. I asked him if he'd spoken to

Munguiko about the bullying and home sickness he experienced when he tried university life in Goma. Indeed, Dieudonne had thought about all this. He presented his own plan B and asked that I pay for him to apprentice to a motor mechanic. He thought he could eventually make a good income with his own roadside business since the village was so close to the main highway west of Goma. Fabien, who had many contacts in the area, found a mechanic willing to take on Dieudonne as an apprentice, and all the necessary tools and fees were paid for him to begin his training.

Figure 8.2: Dieudonne learning to be a mechanic

Kayese had passed the State Finals Examination on his third attempt last year and I had paid for him and Munguiko to study community development at a college in Sake. This meant they could continue living with their families in the village and also support each other in their study. They were going into their second year of the program this year and I hoped they might now begin to show some leadership. Since they were on vacation while I was there, I suggested that they put into practice some of the community organisation skills they had learnt and mobilise the people to clean up the rubbish that littered the village. They set off about this cheerfully enough at first, but when I checked back an hour or so later I found they had disappeared, leaving just one of the frailest of the older men of the village to work on the task. They had at best learnt to delegate! But this man had collected a pile of rubbish and set fire to it in the centre of a row of houses. The women from the houses were furious and protesting as the acrid smoke from the fire polluted the air and their washing.

I was encouraged by the progress of the six women and four men who continued to attend Evelyn's literacy class. They all presented me with little notes in Swahili to show me they were able to read and write. Basic literacy wouldn't mean much in terms of an income for them but it was marvellous for their self-esteem, and all the research suggests a correlation with lower birth rates and better health in a family when women are educated. I spoke to Evelyn about the possibility of four of these young women working in some capacity with the children's program because we needed more staff.

Figure 8.3: The men from the literacy class. All graduates received Swahili Bibles as prizes, but Kanari wanted to show the ball I gave him for the young men's soccer team

Only six of the twenty women who started in the sewing classes persevered, but by this stage these six were competent enough to make fancy outfits for themselves as well as sew all the school uniforms. I was disappointed to learn that Giselle, probably no more than fifteen years old now but looking like a mature woman, had married a man from across the lake in South Kivu and gone to live there. We gave each of the young women who had completed the course their own sewing machine as a graduation present. Many aid programs for rape survivors that I'd seen in Congo and Rwanda provided tailoring classes, but at the end of the training the women were really no better off because they couldn't afford to buy their own sewing machines. All too often short-term aid programs are judged a success because 'x' number of people complete a training program, but the criteria for success and funding stop there and don't explore whether there is a change for the better in the life circumstances of the participants. I could no longer fund the salary of Wamini, our sewing teacher, but she too was content to be awarded her own machine.

Wilfreda, the agronomist, had proved to be a tireless worker and all sixty-five houses had established kitchen gardens funded by my Rotary friends. The cabbages, tomatoes and leeks looked healthy as I walked around the village. I hoped that the women would continue to tend them once Wifreda was no longer employed. She had also set up seedling beds in the grounds of the preschool where she had introduced medicinal plants and herbs and given lessons on these to the children.

***

During my stay, a delegation of men, led by the rather fierce young man called Kanari, came to complain that all my help was for the women – what was I doing for the men? I managed to hold my tongue, and Thomson, from the Anglican Church in Goma, took up the challenge, saying the church had a grant from the USA which could be used to rent land for them to grow cassava, the staple food here. However, they would need their own gardening implements, so I authorised the purchase of machetes and hoes for everyone willing to work. It would be interesting to see how many men had taken up this opportunity when I returned next trip. Remembering the life-threatening wounds a machete can inflict I shuddered at the thought that some of these impulsive and alienated young men were now armed.

Nevertheless, thankful for the cooperation of the Anglican community in Goma, I attended the Anglican Katindo Church in Goma one Sunday. The Reverend Desiree, the rector, was Thomson's brother, and he had told me that two years ago many of the church members and children in the school on the property had narrowly escaped death when mortars had exploded in the grounds of the church. It was only as Samuel drove us off the road to park precariously above a huge deep hole made by the mortars that I understood why the confirmation ceremony last year had been held in our building at Mubambiro. The lava brick walls of the new church were as yet only a few metres high. The church was now meeting in one of the school classrooms but there was no room for many members, who congregated outside the door.

We were ushered inside to reserved seats to hear the preacher for the day. He was a passionate young Congolese man who had just returned from a mission in South Sudan. Most people had already been in the stuffy room for the pre-service hour of singing but he and his team held us all spellbound for another hour with a hilarious performance of the parable of the unjust steward and the theme of forgiveness. There is so much that people have to forgive in Congo! Following the sermon, Arnold, the principal of the school, got up to tell how he had been followed home from the bank a few days ago after withdrawing funds to set up for the new school year. The bandits had taken the money and everything of value in the house – but he gave thanks that they hadn't assaulted or raped any of his family members. Such home invasions are commonplace and I had heard of several incidents where relatives of my friends had been killed. Bandits targeted people like school principals and anyone who regularly picked up cash to pay salaries. This was a risk Samuel took every month, distributing the salaries and paying expenses at Mubambiro. I sent funds in US currency and he paid in this currency because one US dollar was worth one thousand Congolese francs – an impossibly bulky way to do business!

I was anxious to meet Principal Arnold because Evelyn reported that our preschool had recently attracted the attention of the local education authorities. Apparently, they were under the impression that it was a private enterprise, owned by someone called Pamela who was making a profit out of it. With the cooperation of the Revd Desiree and Principal Arnold we were able to register our program for tax exemption with the Anglican school. However, because of the implications of the name we had to remove the sign calling the school 'Pamela's Preschool'. Instead we put up a sign saying 'In Memory of Pamela', and called the building St Mark's Community Centre, in recognition of the financial support from the people at St Mark's Anglican Church South Hurstville in Sydney.

At the preschool this year we had enrolled forty-five children under six years of age, fifteen of them being from the Bantu families nearby in response to the call to integrate the Pygmy and local children. I spent several days with the teachers, trying to introduce alternative methods of discipline as well as ways they could help the children develop age-appropriate physical and cognitive skills. I'd seen Nsii making little children run around the building chasing her in the heat of the day because they were sleepy – an activity reflecting her ideas about physical exercise. I found it frustrating that we couldn't supply even the most basic of play equipment, and very little material was available to use in creative ways. Children often used stones to play 'jacks', and I once saw an older child showing his younger brother how to make a truck, skilfully folding remnants of cardboard boxes and connecting empty cotton reel 'wheels' with fraying string remnants, but these were treasures rarely to be found in the trash in the village. I was horrified when some children improvised balls by blowing up used condoms they found discarded by the UN forces.

In addition to the kitchen gardens, the funds from the friends at the Rotary Club of Rockdale City had paid for a high fence around our St Mark's compound. The fence gave some security, but since we now had so much equipment for the various programs held there, I decided to hire two of the men from the village as guards. I chose Kinubi for one, having observed his hard work during the construction of the village. The second guard, Kanari, was a choice Samuel and I discussed at length. We decided that in this way we might channel his energy into making a positive contribution to the village. It might also be a good thing for his wife and children. We issued the men with the raingear from our forest adventure, as well as boots, mobile phones and torches.

Before I left Goma there was time to renew relationships with special people at HEAL Africa Hospital. I wept with dear Virginie who was facing one more tragic loss in her life. Virginie had fled to Goma some years ago as a new widow with her three young children after her husband had died suddenly and in mysterious circumstances, possibly a politically motivated assassination. She'd found work at HAH and friendship with another young widow in similar circumstances, and they'd set up Amavesa, a mutual support association for widows. Now her children were grown up and she had grandchildren, but almost two years ago during the occupation of the city by the M23, a new-born baby girl with serious congenital internal deformities was abandoned at the hospital. Virginie's tender heart was so moved that she decided to mother this poor child she called Abigael. As it happened, Australian surgeon Neil Wetzig was on hand at the time and performed amazing surgery that allowed her to survive. But only for a time – by this, her second year, her health had deteriorated. I said goodbye to her and heartbroken Virginie on what proved to be just a few days before Abigael's death.

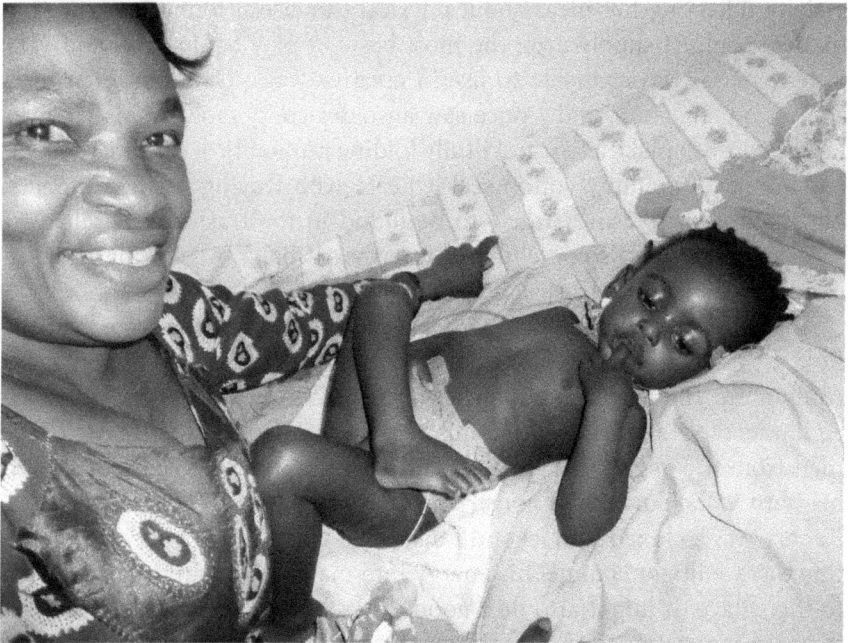

Figure 8.4: Virginie with Abigael

For some time my friends in Australia had been encouraging me to set up a not-for-profit agency in Congo and in Sydney which would be able to appeal publicly for donations that would also be tax deductible. Finally convinced that this was possible and even essential, I spent my last day in Goma this year in meetings to establish the local partner agency we called Pygmy Child Care (PCC), formulate our mission statement and constitution, and decide on the roles and responsibilities of the board members. Samuel was chosen as president and Fabien as secretary; Maitre Martin gave his advice about the legal obligations; the receptionist at the Bungwe with his accounting skills was appointed treasurer. Fabien translated our draft constitution into French, and the board members undertook to negotiate with the authorities to establish our new agency. I would need to go through all this again in Australia for the partner organisation there which would be recognised by the Australian government and fulfil all the requirements for public fund-raising and tax benefits for donors.

***

I arrived in Sydney once again so grateful to have been born in Australia. I caught the eye of my sister-in-law waiting for me as I exited the airport arrivals hall, and I'd gone no more than a few steps when two officers caught up with me and ushered me back inside. While I'd made no secret about where I'd been, the immigration and customs officers who had checked my documents had failed at first to pick up on the fact that Congo was an ebola risk. Probably there aren't many Australians coming back from Congo. Ebola originated in the forests of central Africa, and in the past would wipe out everyone in an isolated village so that outbreaks of the disease would die out. But in today's world, where people can travel around the world and through several countries in a day, the disease has taken hold in urban centres in several African nations, especially Nigeria and Sierra Leone where it had already killed many people. It is now considered a threat to the entire world.

Back inside the airport I was closely questioned and given instructions about what I was to do if I became ill – which was not to go to an emergency room at a hospital where I could spread the deadly virus. Finally, I was released. My long-suffering family were standing at the exit door with anxious looks, wondering if I'd been carted off to an isolation ward. I was eager to show them the sores on my hands and arms where the fire ants had taken pieces out of me, but given what they'd feared while waiting, they weren't all that impressed.

Chapter 9

Stormy weather – November 2015

Thankfully, here is Deo at the exit door of Kigali International Airport, Rwanda to greet me. 'I am *tres malade!*' I say to him. He gives me a hug as I explain that not only am I suffering a severe attack of migraine, but my luggage hasn't arrived with me.

The flashing lights and nauseating pain of this headache had begun even before I was on the plane out of Sydney. I sat in the dark with my eyes closed throughout the fourteen-plus hours of the flight. In Johannesburg, I debated whether I should cancel the flight into Rwanda or force myself to keep going. I decided it was easier to get myself on the plane than to reorganise my travel for the ongoing journeys. Moreover, my precious maroon Samsonite hard-case with all the essentials for my work in Congo and some home comforts such as toilet paper, wet-wipes and sweet biscuits was booked through to Kigali. I had a window seat as we flew just above the clouds over the forests of Central Africa. In appreciative awe, I watched lightning zigzagging across the sky around us and bouncing off the clouds. I really didn't need any more flashing lights this trip, but it was exciting to be so close to such a splendid display of natural wonders – until the person in the seat beside me became quite agitated and assured me it was actually very dangerous!

***

Now we are safely on the ground in Kigali and I can relax and let Deo take over. We make the 'property irregularity report' with RwandAir, hoping the bag will arrive tomorrow, and we set out for Goma. I usually enjoy these four hours driving through Rwanda, where every trip since 2009 I've noticed increasing prosperity and development. But today I just want to get to Goma. The weather is deteriorating by the minute, and as we approach the border with Congo I don't know how Deo can see to drive in the pelting rain. He is as close as he dares to get to the immigration building on the Rwandan side and I can't find the plastic poncho I usually keep in my handbag. I'm just about to step out into the tropical downpour and ankle deep water, but here is Samuel at my side with an umbrella. Bless him. He has come across to shepherd me into Goma. The Congolese border officials make no concessions for the drenched people making the crossing. And although I have already prepaid almost US$500 for my visa approval document, they refuse to stamp the visa in my passport until I hand over another $125. I'm sure this is not legal but it's not worth contesting.

Goma's wet streets are pitch black, and arriving at the Bungwe I know this means no power, no running water, no hot shower. The receptionist is apologetic as he tells me the owner of the Bungwe is here so I can't have my usual little apartment. At least for a night or two I'll be in a room in a block of five where all the other rooms are occupied by military men on leave. I could cry, but I have to change into some dry clothes or I'll be seriously ill very quickly. For the first time in my nine trips to Goma I haven't even put a change of underwear in the small bag I have with me. Poor Samuel suggests I try a shop opposite the public hospital which sometimes stays open at night for patients. He's wet to the skin too, but willingly accompanies me to the shop, which only sells men's clothes. By torchlight, the delighted proprietor finds me a pair of men's pyjamas, underpants and a sweater. I know Samuel has a long, dark, wet and bumpy drive home to his two-roomed timber cabin with a dirt floor and plastic sheets lining the walls to keep out the rain. My room at the Bungwe wouldn't rate two stars on an international scale, but it is weatherproof and has indoor plumbing when there is water and a somewhat comfortable bed.

***

I'd hoped I would only need to wear these men's clothes for a day, but the bag that went missing didn't arrive until a few days before I was due to go home. Had I known it would take that long I could have had a seamstress make me several Congolese outfits before then. My dear brother in Sydney called Qantas, and Innocent badgered RwandAir in Kigali, but no one could say where the maroon bag was until it finally turned up in Kigali. No one would pay compensation for the added costs I'd incurred in getting it delivered to Goma – so much for travel insurance!

After a couple of days into my visit and still no sign of my luggage, Samuel took me to Goma's only women's ready-to-wear clothing emporium. Most of the stock was kept up three flights of steep stairs, with no windows, no air, no light, no change room. They put me between two clothes racks with

Samuel at the end guarding my modesty as I tried to get into impossibly tight hipster jeans, again by torchlight. I was told modern Congolese girls who can afford them wear these jeans to make rape more difficult. But they weren't for me and it was with relief that at last I found a tracksuit that fitted and have had to be content wearing that, even though by the light of day it turned out to be a truly shocking pink. It took days for my own sodden clothes to dry in the humid air of a wet, wet season.

***

I had two major concerns for this trip. First was the maintenance of the building we now called St Mark's Community Centre. This issue was closely related to the second concern: the programs for the youngest children. The building now housed so many of the development projects we'd been implementing, and especially the child-care activities, but its maintenance had been a steep learning curve for me as well as an unwelcome expense. Every year I'd had to pay to replace broken windows, repaint the interior and resurface the floor. The colonel who'd commandeered the building in 2013 had made holes in the cement floor to store his supply of explosives. Although the holes were filled in when we got it back, I suspected the repairs were made with inferior cement mix because the patched areas regularly broke down and were a tripping hazard for children and adults. Also, lacking experience in building projects, I hadn't noticed that there were no gutters on the building when it was constructed – until the wet season arrived and I saw the tropical downpour cascading off the roof. But even with gutters and downpipes channelling the rain into two huge water tanks, the excessive runoff remained a problem. The lava that flowed from the volcano and formed the land here was impenetrable. Rainwater stayed on the surface looking for an escape, pooling in any depression with giant puddles forming in front of the building. Since it all dried up when the rains stopped around April there was a reluctance to do much about it.

As far as the broken windows were concerned I called our guards, Kinube and Kanari, to explain why I should continue to pay them when our property was regularly damaged. I was horrified to see how thin and sick Kinube looked. I sent him to HAH where tests revealed he had tuberculosis. Of course, he could not continue to work at the centre where he could infect the children, but I paid for his continuing treatment, hoping he would take the medications as long as necessary. Kanari was a different story – it turned out that he found guard duty to be 'women's work' and had been sending Yvette, his pregnant wife, to sit in the cold outside the building every night. I felt sorry for Yvette but dismissed Kanari and hired a replacement, a young man called Byakweli whose house was just behind the centre.

Last year I'd decided that since I had limited resources, my focus would have to be on the health and nutrition program for the youngest children. They are the future of the community, and the first seven years of life are crucial in their physical, mental and social development. This visit I came with a video made by a filmmaker, Dale Kim, at St Mark's Preschool in South Hurstville, Sydney. Staff, parents and children had cooperated in the making of the video which demonstrated how activities to develop basic verbal, numerical, physical and social skills could be taught through play. In Congo we lacked the purpose-built facility and equipment in the Australian school, but the teachers could see the possibilities for adopting some of the games, and they remarked on how the Australian children were just like Congolese children in so many ways.

The film also demonstrated the way teachers at St Mark's maintained order and developed independence with games and songs. And especially how children were happy to wash, and even to eat, in relays, rather than having to wait until everyone was served their meal. Of course, very few children in Australia live with the prolonged hunger which is the norm for the Pygmy children. The little ones in the Pygmy village have to be quick to get a mouthful of the meagre, irregular meals served in their families. Since they now know that no one eats at the centre until everyone is served they are spared that anxiety.

Despite these programs to improve the general health and wellbeing of the youngest members of the village, I was surprised and confused one day as I walked around the village to see so many little children who looked sick and undernourished. Nsii assured me that she had enrolled all of our Pygmy children under six years in the program and that the children I had noticed belonged to displaced families camping temporarily in the village. This did turn out to be partly true. But when an Australian–Congolese friend who worked with medical programs in African countries visited the village, he discovered that the number of local Bantu children far exceeded the Pygmy children benefiting from the program, and that in fact they all had to pay fees.

On further investigation, I discovered that it was not altogether Nsii's fault. She'd been visited again by local education authorities who pressured her to charge fees from which they took a percentage, and most of the Pygmy families had no cash to spare for school fees. I knew that the primary and high schools paid part of their fees to the local education department. One possible explanation was that it covered in-service training for teachers in the rural areas, who mostly had no other formal training. But these revelations about fees also brought to light the fact that my concept of our preschool as a safe place for the youngest children to be provided with food, health care and play activities was totally at odds with the expectations of the local education authorities. For them, our program was a school which was under their jurisdiction where the children had to acquire advanced skills in reading, writing and arithmetic. Nsii was under pressure for the children to perform, so the poorest and youngest of our children were excluded from the program!

Given all this, I saw an opportunity to completely change the nature of the program. The current staff continued in employment until the end of the year when severance was legal. Then Evelyn took over as coordinator of the Pygmy Child Care program. Her new staff comprised four of the Pygmy women who had completed the literacy classes: Natalie, Chance, Chantal and Solange. The changes in staff reflected the changed nature of the work. We no longer had a preschool, so we didn't need teachers. We had a child-care program exclusively for the youngest Pygmy children so we had carers from the Pygmy community. The program in 2016 for around eighty children included a maternal and child health aspect where pregnant and breast-feeding mothers would be given food and medical checks; a feeding program of porridge for children aged from eighteen months to three years; and a program of educational activities, daily meals and health care for children aged from three to seven years.

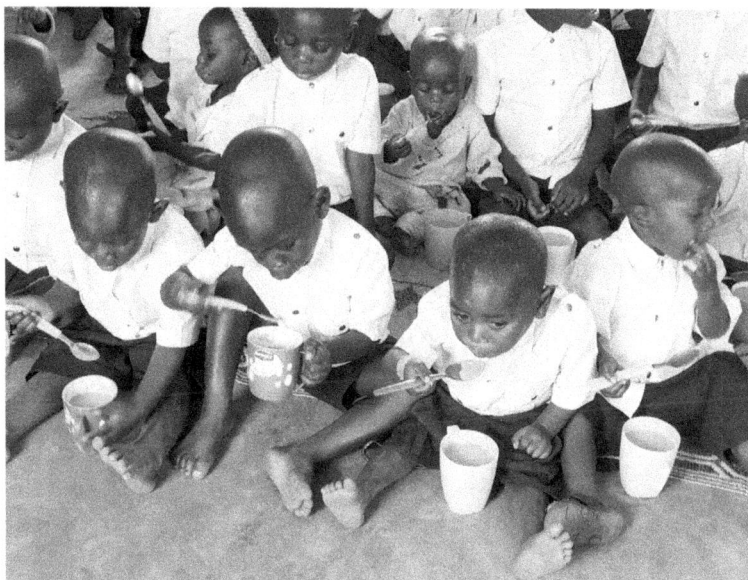

Figure 9.1: Porridge every day for children under three years

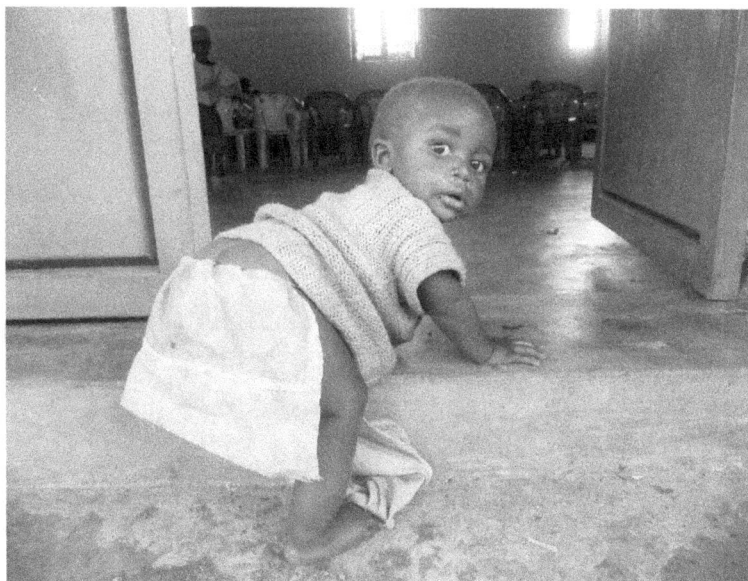

Figure 9.2: Children must be able to walk to be admitted to our program but some can't wait

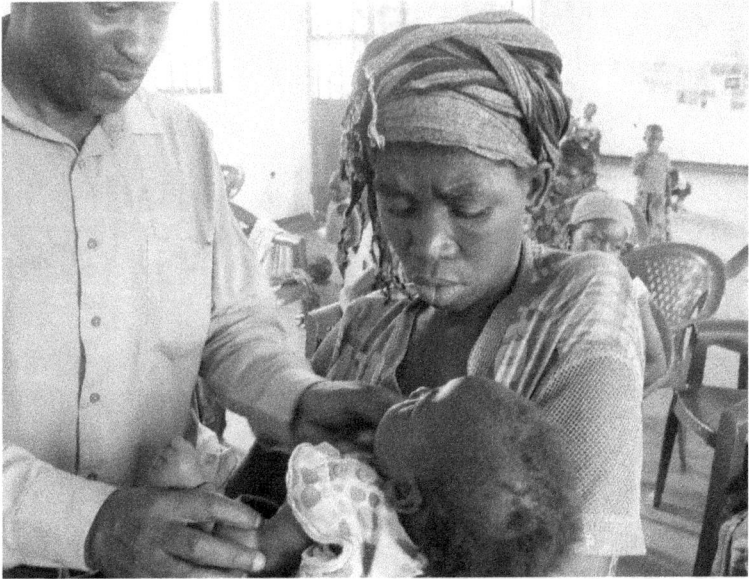

Figure 9.3: Fabien conducts maternal and child health clinics once a month

Figure 9.4: Educational activities – children learning to hold a pencil and write their names

Although I have many people in Australia who are generous with their financial support, I realised earlier this year that the paperwork involved in setting up and operating a charity in Australia to partner Pygmy Child Care in Congo was more than I could manage without a committed team of volunteers. Since then, I'd been seeking to link with an existing agency approved by the Australian Tax Office and the Department of Foreign Affairs and Trade to manage and fund overseas projects. After a lot of consultation, I was drawn to partnering with an Australian-founded non-government organisation, headquartered in Australia, called Global Development Group (GDG). My friends in the medical teams that volunteered at HAH were already in partnership with GDG and were very satisfied with the relationship. The paperwork to partner with GDG was daunting, but I was given all the help I needed and the partnership began at the end of 2016.

I would continue to raise the $1500 each month that covered the salaries of the workers, the health and nutrition programs for all the children under seven years of age and the pregnant women. GDG would receive all donations, handle the transfer of funds to Congo every month, issue receipts to donors who wanted to claim tax deductions, liaise as necessary with Australian Government agencies, submit our six-monthly reports to these agencies, make on-site visits to check on and mentor local partners, and maintain an information page on their website.

***

With the child-care program the focus of activities this year, I reasoned that it was time to cut back on infrastructure and development funds for the village. For five years now, the Good Men and I had consulted with the people in the village and provided advice and support for their transition to a settled way of life. A lot of money had been invested in the various training and income-generating projects over these years. Unfortunately, only a minority of people had been able to follow through with the projects. Realistically, it was too short a time-span for most of the adults to make all the enormous adjustments they faced in resettlement. It wasn't just the shift from living in the forest. That was made years ago, but since then, until quite recently when the village was built, people had lived as nomads and beggars. For some, this way of life had become the norm.

However, my resolve to confine financial support to the child-care program was tested when I learnt that cholera, always endemic in the region, was this year in epidemic proportions throughout the country, the worst in fifteen years. I was persuaded that the existing pit-toilets, painstakingly dug behind each house, weren't deep enough and were contributing to the spread of the disease, so I agreed to fund two substantial lava-brick communal pit-toilet blocks in two locations in the village. Fabien would conduct a 'sensitisation' session with residents to ensure the toilets were kept clean and to encourage people to wash their hands after using them.

Figure 9.5: The leading men: at the back Mubawa, in front Kayese, Alexis, Munguiko and Kanari. Note they have put up a sign acknowledging the aid provided by the Australian Government

Before I left Goma, I had to face one more distressing revelation. Sixteen-year-old Florence was the only girl in the village who had completed primary education. While most parents agreed that they wanted their children to have an education, they also expected even quite young children to contribute by undertaking various chores.

In Florence's case I paid fees for her to study at high school and in exchange she helped at the preschool with chores such as preparing meals and washing dishes and cooking pots. She was very teachable and clever. She sat in on the children's activities and the literacy classes whenever possible and even joined in on the sewing lessons so she learnt to use the machines as proficiently as any of the other women in the class. Mid-year, for more than a week, Florence was missing and presumed to have been kidnapped by rebels and taken to the forest. Her family were distraught and Thomson came to the village to hold prayer vigils for her safety and release. But then her family revealed that her clothes and various gifts I'd given her were also missing. Finally, we learnt that she had gone to a prearranged assignation with an officer in the nearby army camp. In fact, they'd organised what passes for a marriage. Her parents were furious since the man hadn't made the customary visit to get their blessing, nor had he offered the *mali* (bride price). I began to suspect that this omission was their main concern, given that as a pretty and accomplished young woman she should have brought them a goat at the very least. I couldn't blame her for hoping she might have a better future with an army officer than with a penniless Pygmy, but I wondered if he would take her with him when he was inevitably moved on from Mubambiro or if she would find herself pregnant and abandoned like other young women in the village.

Figure 9.6: A four-year-old boy guarding the vegetable patch from marauding goats

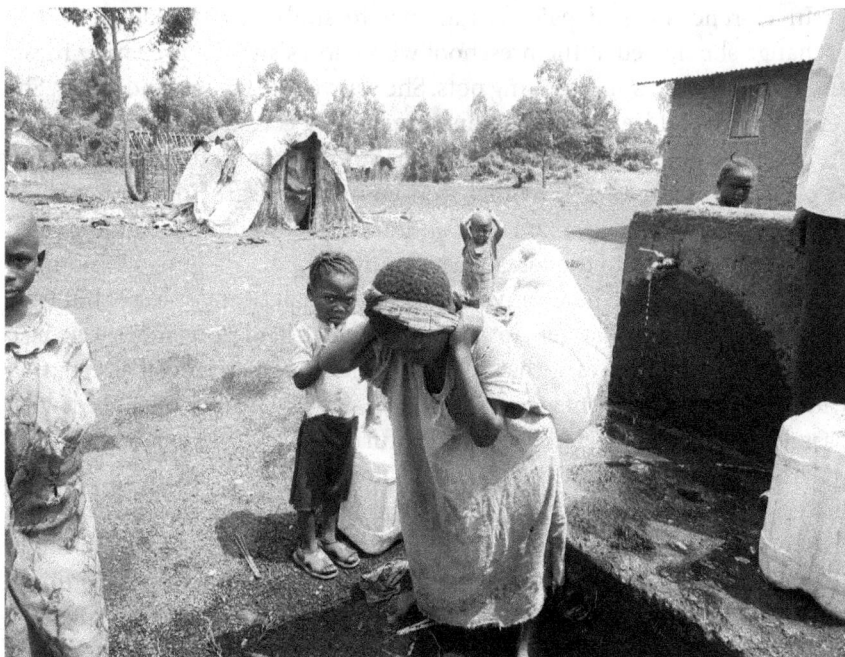

Figure 9.7: Fetching water is a back-breaking task for young girls

***

After so many dramas this trip I was looking forward to an uneventful trip home. But even as we left Goma we drove into violent thunderstorms and pouring rain. As we sped through one heavily wooded area, Deo cheerfully told me that this time last year a hundred people had died here in a storm. The good thing from his point of view was that the police, remembering this, would be taking shelter elsewhere so he didn't have to worry about being fined for speeding.

In Kigali, it was still raining and no planes could land or take off until the storm eased. Over the years, I'd seen dramatic changes in the airport. On my second visit, while waiting for a flight to Kenya via Bujumbura scheduled to fly out at 1 a.m., I spoke to the only other passenger in the departure lounge. He was an airline crash investigator who took great pleasure in explaining why the terminal was a construction site. Just months before, an incoming RwandAir flight had overshot the runway and ploughed into the building.

With this in mind it was a relief when we took off that night about an hour ahead of schedule. Why not, when all of the listed passengers were present? This year, although we sat in a thoroughly modern facility, all the latest innovations in the new building were small compensation for me and the crowd of cold, tired, bored travellers waiting for our flight to leave.

When the plane from South Africa finally came in and was quickly prepared for the turnaround trip, the schedule was changed to include a stop in Lusaka, Zambia. It was 2.30 a.m. when I finally checked in at the hotel in Johannesburg, South Africa. They thought I'd cancelled and I had to wait while they prepared another room for me. I fell into a troubled sleep only to be woken at 5 a.m. by banging somewhere nearby. An hour later they were cleaning my windows and shortly after that there was a fire drill. At least I revelled in a long hot shower after so many days without running water at the Bungwe. I was sure things would look up once I was on the way home to Australia on the 'big red flying kangaroo'. We were all prepared for take-off when the captain announced a delay because a red light connected to the fuelling system wouldn't go off. So we sat on the tarmac for an hour and a half while that problem was resolved. Once we were in the air I refused dinner so that I could try to get some sleep.

Somewhere over Antarctica the captain called for any doctors on board to come to the aid of a seriously ill passenger. At first it seemed the patient wouldn't survive and it was suggested we would need to land in Perth. But she rallied and we made it to Melbourne where the transfer to hospital and then the refuelling delayed us another hour and a half. By that stage I had missed four meals and longed to be home, but I was very impressed by the efforts of the Qantas crew to save the woman's life. We were the only plane coming into Sydney by the time we landed many hours late, and were hastened through the formalities. I'd booked the maroon bag through from Kigali to Sydney but didn't care if I ever saw it again. Ironically, when the carousel sprang into action, it was the first bag to emerge.

Chapter 10

Feed the hungry, heal the sick, take care of the little children – March 2017

'Oh Ferdie!' I struggle to disguise my shock and distress. The once sturdy, self-assured little man lies prone on the dirt floor, a shadow of himself. This is a man I really respect. He hasn't sat around in the village drinking home brew, bemoaning the past and depending on his wife to feed him and his children. He and Vumilia have worked together to make a decent life. They have taken pride in their home and their kitchen gardens. He has set a good example for the boys growing up in the village, especially his sons. Now I fear he is dying.

It is sixteen months since my last visit and I wonder if I could have saved him if only I'd come back sooner. His eyes are bright, feverish, and his breath catches. He tells me it all started a few months ago. 'I was just walking along when suddenly there was a terrible pain in my back and I fell down. Ever since then my legs are no good.' 'Can you move at all?' I want to know. Vumilia, who has just given birth to their sixth child, Foster, a healthy little boy at her breast, replies, 'Only with two of us helping.' She shakes her head sadly. Ferdie's mates, who were sitting with him when I arrived, shift around for Chantal, the eldest of Ferdie and Vumilia's children, to place a stool for me to sit on. Ferdie points to his chest – he has a lot of pain there, too, and he has difficulty eating. We chat briefly. I tell him I have some medicine which might help ease the pain and will leave it with Chantal.

Apparently, efforts were made to persuade Ferdie to go to HAH months ago for treatment. But he refused, asking instead for money to buy a goat. The witch doctor had promised he could make him walk again if he had a goat to sacrifice. I'm not really surprised by this. I know that some folk have abandoned the witch doctor and his various charms as well as traditional medicines since Thomson has been holding Christian meetings in the centre. However, I also know that old customs die hard. Rose's little girl, Aimee, wore the witch doctor's necklace of feathers to cure the fungus that was eating away her face until she went to HAH for antibiotics; Alexis tells me his painful knees and ankles are cursed so they are covered by tiny black tattoos made with the heated prongs of a fork dipped in ashes. Staff at the Bungwe told of applying something called a 'black stone', actually a piece of blackened cow bone, to cure a child when he was bitten by a snake late one night and it was too dangerous to try to get him to medical help. I know some traditional remedies may be effective but it is distressing that in several instances I've heard of people dying because they depended on the witch doctor's expensive and ineffective remedies until it was too late for modern medicine that would have saved them.

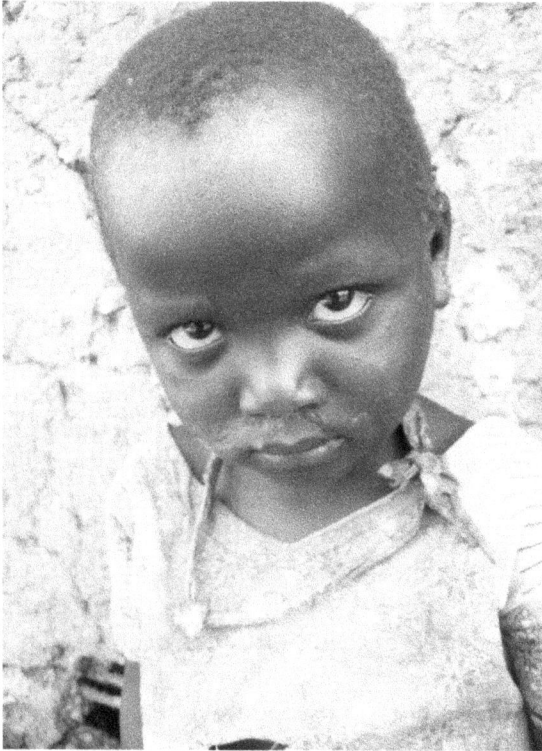

Figure 10.1: Aimee wearing the necklace of feathers and rag prescribed by the witch doctor to cure a fungal infection on her face

Fortunately, Chantal graduated from Evelyn's literacy program over a year ago and has been working with her in the child-care program ever since. Her salary is now supporting the entire family – they are living on no more than $5 a week. I ask her about twelve-year old Muhindo, the oldest boy: 'Is he still going to school?' Chantal responds, 'He goes when he can be spared but most days now he must replace our father and work as a delivery boy in the market.' After five years on the rough roads, the bike they bought with the initial income-generating grant needs major repairs. I give her funds for a new bike for the boy, knowing that more than likely some of it will buy a goat – and hope for a dying man.

It would probably be painful, fruitless and costly to get Ferdie to HAH, even if he agreed. He is at least thirty-six years old, which is around the normal lifespan of Pygmies in the forest. He has worked hard carrying huge, heavy loads on his back, and more recently on his bike, all his life, always on the verge of starvation. I wonder if perhaps his bones have just collapsed. The medical advice I've received since suggests it may be that he has tuberculosis in the bones, or alternatively that his bones and kidneys have been affected by the level of minerals, especially excess fluoride, in the local water, which is heavily contaminated by volcanic runoff.

***

I was only in Congo for eight days this time. I'd had to delay my travel again and again in 2016 due to the security situation. News of the sporadic violence in Congo, which was rarely reported in Australia, had filtered in to me every so often when it impacted on the lives of my friends. For example, Fabien's father had been caught in crossfire and killed after braving the danger to go to a market for food for the family. The presidential elections which were originally scheduled for November 2015 had been delayed and rescheduled for November 2016. But by then the Congolese President would have passed the end of his third five-year term in office, and generally in the eastern provinces people were afraid he would again cancel the elections. Discontent fuelled by this expected betrayal, and the possibility of increased violent suppression of opposition, led HAH to advise that volunteers should not visit in the last half of the year, making an exception for the Australian surgeon Neil Wetzig. His extraordinary surgical and teaching skills were always an asset and would be particularly so when the hospital could well be overrun with casualties.

The major civil war people feared didn't happen despite the anticipated cancellation of elections, and early in 2017 my friends advised me that it might be safe for me to return. I always register with the government website <smartraveller.gov.au> before I leave Australia. As usual, the directive for travel to Eastern Congo this trip was 'Do Not Travel'. However, I was alarmed on the eve of my departure when I received a message from the nearest (but not very near) Australian diplomatic mission in Harare, Zimbabwe, warning against ignoring this advice. That was a first. I decided to travel anyway because my friends always tell me my visits give them hope and encouragement that the world hasn't forgotten them.

This trip I took the northern route with Qatar Airways for the first time and found it very comfortable – until I boarded the aircraft from Doha to Kigali. A day into the journey from Sydney, flying in a crowded plane with low ceilings and, I suspect, the air-conditioning turned off, I had my first experience of a panic attack. I couldn't breathe and thought I would pass out. I clambered over the enormous man beside me and ran up to the cabin crew, who were horrified when I demanded, 'I have to get off this plane.' Fortunately, I was eventually able to laugh at myself, always a good remedy for panic. A crew member gave me water and said we would soon be landing at Entebbe and most of the passengers would disembark there, so I managed to cope with the rest of the flight, vowing always to book an aisle seat in the future. After I spent a night in Kigali, my friends assured me that it was safe for me to travel on into Congo.

***

Ferdie's plight was a sad beginning to my tenth visit to Congo. However, there was a lot to cheer me when I walked around the village that first day. Smiling mothers came to show off healthy babies – a result of the maternal and child health clinics. Every month, pregnant and breast-feeding women were receiving food and pre- and post-natal care. In the past, when I arrived I would be besieged by anxious mothers waiting for me, begging me to see what could be done for their ailing infants. And I remember one year meeting a pregnant young woman on the road who looked like her baby would be arriving any minute. I asked her when the baby was due and she replied angrily, 'How would I know – ask God.' A few years ago I heard a statistic that one in every thirteen women in Congo die in childbirth, and I know a high number of women suffer life-changing birth trauma because of lack of peri-natal care. Whatever the situation among the Pygmies in the past, now the monthly checks at the clinic were helping women to be prepared for the birth.

Figure 10.2: A proud mother with her healthy baby

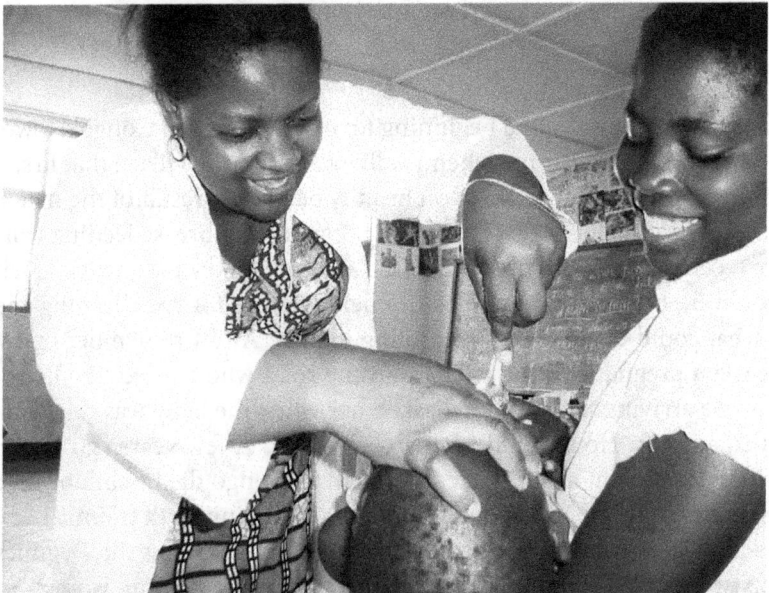

Figure 10.3: Fabien's wife Bahati, midwife at HAH, also helps at the clinic

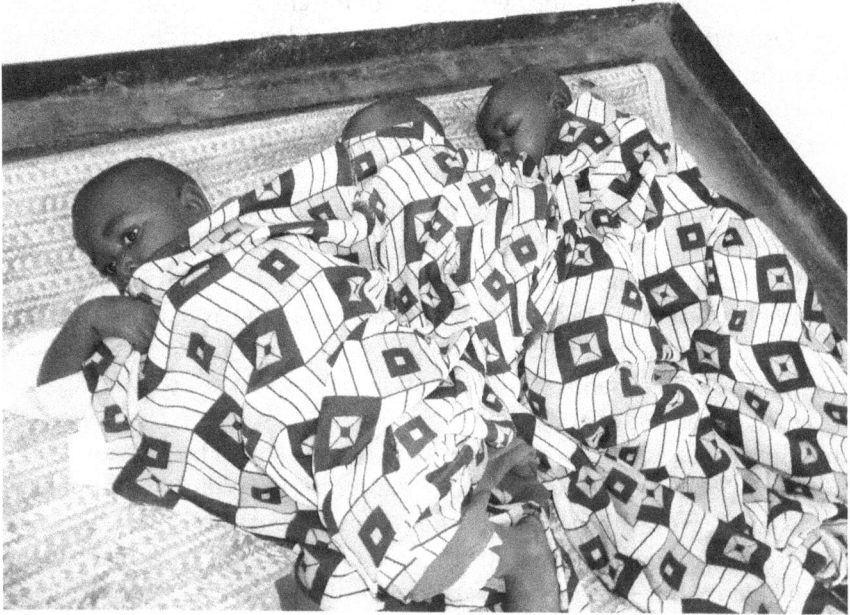

Figure 10.4: Nap time for the youngest children

In the St Mark's centre I took photos of the toddlers, some being fed and others helping themselves with spoon and mug to a quite tasty and definitely nutritious porridge of sweetened mixed grains. The children under three years of age sat on a mat at the front and joined in the activities of the older children as much as they could, while the youngest lay down under covers to take a nap.

I observed Chantal, Chance, Solange and Natalie as they worked with the children. Chantal played the drum for many of the activities. Her voice was sweet, clear and powerful as she led traditional songs. The children were happy, engaged; no one was threatening them with a stick to keep them in order. A child cried and Evelyn comforted him. It was so different from the atmosphere in past years. The carers were now part of the village, they knew and loved the children, and the children knew and trusted them, their sisters, cousins and aunties. In the formal learning activities for the children who were three years and up, Evelyn had adapted some of the methods demonstrated in the film made at St Mark's Preschool. The children were proud to show that they could write their names – totally absorbed in the effort as they wrestled with the chalk.

Most of the lessons were in Swahili. However, French is the other official language in Eastern Congo, and when they go to school, these children will have to study in French. Evelyn called out a group of children and assigned roles. They then played a scene where one child and his friends met another on the way to school. In confident French they exchanged greetings, their names and what they were doing and introduced their friends and family. I knew that this ability to communicate in French would be an advantage for them later on when they would be sitting in a classroom of a hundred children and trying to take advantage of the education available to them.

Before they ate the daily meal, they stood to sing a little song about the need to wash their hands, and went off in pairs to do so. They still all ate together. It was a special day due to my visit so they enjoyed a meal of fish in a chilli sauce with *fufu*, a cassava- based equivalent of bread and a staple in the Congolese diet. Most often at the centre the children ate cabbage or cassava leaves with beans, rice, *fufu* or sweet potato; fish or eggs were rare treats. To me *fufu* has all the flavour of glue, and I can't manage the hot *pilipili* (chilli) sauce that is served with it and perhaps makes it more palatable. With the five women working together, the preparation and serving of the meal wasn't as chaotic as in the early days, and the children were now familiar with the routine.

Last year when Fabien began to measure and weigh all the children under six years of age in the village, he discovered ten who were so seriously malnourished that they were officially diagnosed as having the life-threatening condition called kwashiorkor. Four of them who were close to death were taken to a special clinic in Goma for intravenous feeding but three of the children died within a few days, two from the same family. They'd only been discovered because of a door-to-door canvassing of the village checking on all children eligible to come to PCC. Their mother, gaunt and in rags herself, explained that they had no clothes so she had never sent them to the centre. The seven other children who had survived kwashiorkor were still being given special protein-rich meals every day. When malnourished children come down with what might be a minor illness in an otherwise healthy child, the condition is potentially fatal. Sadly, still, for some of the parents the rapid onset of an illness is evidence that the child has been cursed, and the only remedy they trust is that provided by the witch doctor.

Figure 10.5: When the primary school children came to see me at the centre, they were very happy when I gave each of them a cake of soap

While I was with the child-care program, the fourteen children we were sending to primary school and the four in high school came to the centre. Evelyn was the on-site supervisor for the school program, too. She had taught them a song to greet me, which they sang with gusto. For Christmas last year I'd sent funds for all of the children in our program to have two uniforms and a pair of sandals so that they had a change of clean clothes. Most Pygmy families had no cash to buy clothes, especially for children – they were dressed in cast-offs already worn out by older members of the family, and they would wear the same old clothes day and night until they were dirty rags. Evelyn was trying to teach all of the children to take care of their clothes by organising washing days for them at the centre. This was most important for the children in school because if they arrived in dirty clothes they'd be sent home. I looked at our primary school children and could see that now, in late March, some of them were already out-growing their clothes. There were always more needs to be met if I had the funds.

The child-care program was shut down for the rest of the week for the carers to go to Goma for some training in the newly completed banquet hall at the Bungwe. It was furnished with incongruous red-brocade upholstered, gilt-edged chairs, but we had lots of room and privacy, as well as equipment for me to show films. I thought that the carers might enjoy seeing some of the photos I'd taken in the village over the years and began with photos from 2010 of the very first meeting when they were still in the camp. They cried and pointed as they recognised many of the old people who had danced with me on that day and had since died – the generation who'd been forced from the forest on Mount Shove and all that was familiar. Equally sad for me was their response when I showed the film I'd taken of the gorilla family in the forest. Except for Evelyn, these young women had no memory of the deep forest and they could hardly believe that this was their Congo. The training for the PCC staff included some basic material about child physical and cognitive development, methods of discipline, and how to use pictures and stories to develop language, creativity, social skills and empathy for other people.

Figure 10.6: Evelyn and her team

Under the guidelines for aid programs approved by the Australian Government, our agency had to have a policy on child protection and children's rights, and the training began with this topic. I knew that human rights in general was a subject of major importance for the Pygmy population, once widely regarded in the country as being less than human. Legislation to protect them had been introduced in the Congolese Parliament in 2013, but as far as I knew had never been passed. The possibility of being discriminated against arose whenever Pygmies had to interact with mainstream institutions. Although Pygmies were thought to be the first people of this region, the concept of indigenous rights had few advocates. In other provinces, especially where the forest people were involved on the waterways, they'd been given some formal role in conservation of the environment in recognition of their traditional custodianship. But there was no recognition of traditional rights and responsibilities for the Pygmies of Mubambiro and the Virunga National Park close to the Rwandan border. They were exiled, with no real compensation or alternative for surviving in a settled community.

'And what about protection for women and women's rights!' the women asked when I raised the issue of child protection. They shook their heads about what had happened to Colette. She had raised a few hens from chicks. Her husband had made off with one of these precious birds and come home drunk, with nothing to show for the money, at least US$8 that he would have got for it. When Colette accused him of wasting money that would have fed the family for a week or more, he punched her in the mouth, knocking out several front teeth. Colette, a very pretty young woman, is now permanently disfigured, and the loss of front teeth will impact her health for the rest of her life. Women have no redress for rape or for the domestic violence so many experience daily. On a positive note, the young carers all agreed that since they had these permanent jobs and a salary to buy soap to wash themselves and their clothes, they all felt that their status in the village had gone up several notches, and they had better options for marriage.

In this climate of trust and understanding I was able to ask about some of the women and young girls whose fate worried me. It was a relief to hear that Giselle and her child were safe and well and still living with her husband across the lake in South Kivu. And Florence, too, had a better outcome than I had feared. Her husband had taken her and their child with him when his unit was sent 400 kilometres north to Beni, and when the conflict in that area increased and an outbreak of Ebola erupted, he had sent her to Goma and provided for her and the child to live well there, from where she was often able to visit her mother in Mubambiro. Nevertheless, both of these young women from the Pygmy village were dependent on the goodwill of their husbands, and to a large extent on his family if he died. It bothered me that none of the girls in the village had even completed primary school: this condemned them to a life of poverty and insecurity. Parents wanted education for their children, although more so for sons than daughters. But when labour was needed for household duties, child care or when extra hands were needed to gather seasonal fruits and nuts from the forest verge, education took second place and the children abandoned school.

***

The PCC annual general meeting was scheduled for the day after the training, so Evelyn stayed on at the Bungwe by herself to attend. I thought she might be lonely on her own and would want her sister or one of the other women to stay with her, but she was only too pleased to have a room of her own for the night, a real bed and mattress, an en suite with running water, and meals she didn't have to find and prepare herself.

As our first board had been set up in 2014, new office-bearers were due to be elected this year. Fabien was elected president; Thomson, vice-president; Mama Virginie, public relations and liaison with HAH. Evelyn represented the centre staff and a group of four Pygmy men represented the village residents. Maitre Martin continued as our legal consultant, Samuel as pastoral consultant and Jean Bizi as engineer and building maintenance. The receptionist from the Bungwe continued as manager in the village and secretary and treasurer.

Fabien's report on the maternal and child health program was impressive. He referred to the record books where he kept note of every child under seven years in the village, and their monthly health status, height and weight gain, as well as the number and nature of illnesses he treated for all people in the village every month. Of course, malaria, typhoid, cholera, respiratory diseases and intestinal parasites still afflicted a lot of people, but they were all being treated for their ailments rather than having to suffer stoically. Children in the child-care program who needed surgery or acute care were being taken to HAH. One of the case histories illustrated the difference that PCC programs were making in the lives of individual children. A young mother, Penina, had come to the clinic with her infant son who had been born with two club feet, a condition that would have been a severe disability in a village where the ground was rough and uneven and everyday life involved so much walking. This condition is prevalent in Eastern Congo and warrants research into possible causes: genetic, environmental or dietary. In response to the high incidence of cases coming to HAH, the hospital now had a program to intervene early, at the stage when the child is just learning to walk. Because Penina's son was identified in infancy, he'd been treated over a period of months and could now walk without difficulty.

It was all very encouraging until we came to general business and Maitre Martin had news to destroy my complacency about the village. According to the documents lodged with the Lands Office in 2011, we had a limited time in which to 'improve' the land. Basically, that meant erecting substantial buildings on it. Apparently the clay huts didn't qualify as improvements, and our centre and the new toilets weren't sufficient improvement to cover the 2.5-acre village, so the villagers were up for thousands of dollars in taxes and in danger of the state repossessing the land. The situation was absurd because the land was obviously home to several hundred people who lived in dwellings comparable to the local standard and who would otherwise be camping on the roadside. I wondered if this tax was partly a way to raise money for underpaid public servants who couldn't manage on their unreliable government salaries. We discussed ways of complying without having to pay out a lot of money; even building a substantial fence around parts of the village might be sufficient. I also suspected that strategies to avoid this tax explained all the partially completed buildings I'd seen in and around Goma year after year. Landowners who didn't have enough funds to immediately complete a project could at least show their intention to improve the site by setting foundations. For seven years a three-storey hotel had been under construction beside the Bungwe, but the banquet hall we were using was the only section completed.

My visa would expire before we could come up with solutions to these problems. At least I had first-hand information and an understanding that could only be gained face-to-face when communication was limited by language and cultural differences, and unreliable internet and telephone systems.

As for the predicted danger of this Congo visit, the only risks I took were on the road. Leaving the Bungwe every day, Neville, my driver, had to make three detours taking us almost an hour just to get out of the city centre. In fact, I noticed that the city's outer limits were extending into what had once been sparsely populated open land. Coming back from the village on the first day, Neville negotiated around a total of four overturned trucks – their contents ruined and strewn across the road, a danger to all travellers. On another day, just short of Mugunga, we came up to what at first looked like a demonstration but turned out to be onlookers crowding at the site of an accident between a motorcycle and a truck, with the three people on the motorcycle dead. I'm constantly concerned for the safety of the Good Men, who regularly make this difficult trip to Mubambiro on a motorcycle or in an overcrowded minibus. Most of the minibuses boast messages such as 'Jesus Saves' and 'Trust in God', possibly because when you get in them you're putting life and limb at risk.

On my last day in the village we were in Neville's shiny new Toyota. He had hoped to have it for me for the entire trip because he knew how hard it was for me to climb in and out of the old high vehicle that he used to drive. But the new Toyota didn't arrive until we were making the last trip out of the city, and it still only had international licence plates. The police in Goma held us up for ages debating whether or not he could drive it at all. At the last road block before Mubambiro there was a new officer on duty. I'm sure when I drove up, a rich *mzungu mzee* in my new car, he saw an unmissable opportunity to make some money. I maintained a disinterested expression as Neville argued with him.

Finally, Neville turned to me, 'He wants your passport. I told him this is stupid. How could you get this far from the border without a passport and valid visa? What will we do?' The Good Men, who were in the car with us, were despairing because they knew my passport was securely locked away in the office at the Bungwe. I smiled sweetly at the officer, reached into my bag and handed him a copy of the front page of my passport and the page with my valid entry visa. I always carried these papers after having an unpleasant incident on an earlier visit. He scrutinised the paper for a long time before handing it back.

All too soon it was time to leave Congo. I was once again at the chaotic border by 5 p.m. It was worse than ever because both Congo and Rwanda were building new immigration and customs centres. I was sure it would be a great improvement, when and if they finished. I feared this might be my last visit and it was a tearful farewell with the men who were the sons I never had. As I stumbled my way through no-man's-land it began to rain. I pulled out my little one dollar transparent plastic poncho and tugged it over my head and shoulders. I knew I was about to present the Rwandan border guards with a dilemma: plastic bags are banned in Rwanda and this flimsy cover looked suspiciously like a modified bag. For some moments the officers huddled together and debated whether it was a plastic bag or an item of clothing. In the end, they all laughed and good-naturedly agreed that I could keep it to get me to the shelter of Deo's waiting car.

Chapter 11

Dancing with the Pygmies – April 2019

From the moment I set foot on the tarmac at the small civilian airport in Goma, it is evident that the city is on ebola alert. In Singapore I'd boarded Ethiopian Airlines, which now flies directly into Goma from Addis Ababa via Entebbe, so this visit I arrived in Congo just thirty-two hours after setting out from Sydney. Before travellers can even enter the airport-terminal building we have our first experience of the ubiquitous loudspeakers warning the population, 'Ebola! Ebola!' The super-enthusiastic ebola-control team members check temperatures and supervise the thorough washing of hands at taps set in huge drums of heavily chlorinated water. At the entrance to HEAL Africa Hospital one day on this trip I'm taken to task for not washing with enough vigour, trying to spare my poor hands which are by then red raw!

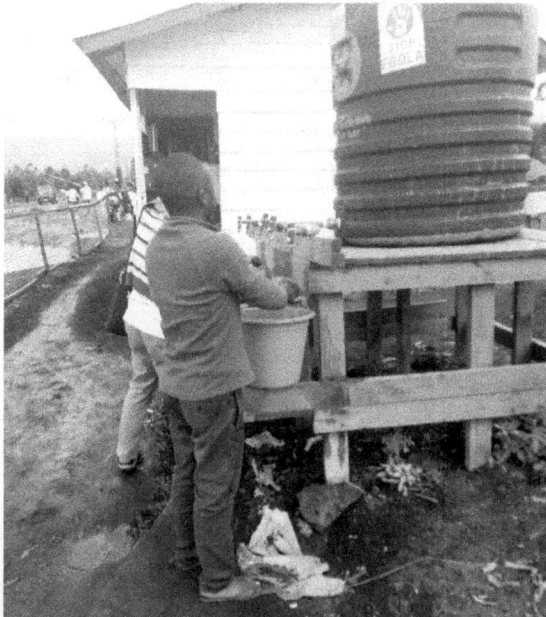

Figures 11.1: Ebola checkpoint on the road to Mubambiro

Ebola has taken more than fourteen hundred lives in North Kivu in the past twelve months but as far as authorities can know it has not at this point reached Goma. Disinformation about ebola is widespread, and although a vaccine is now available for the population in affected areas, many people refuse to have it. Some people believe the virus has been deliberately spread by the government in Kinshasa, or that the threat of increased danger of infection if people assemble in close contact was used as an excuse to deny people in the eastern provinces the chance to vote in the presidential elections last year. As a result, vaccination teams have been attacked and two Medecins Sans Frontieres clinics were burnt down in March, so that agency, in the forefront of the fight to control the epidemic, has suspended its work. During my stay in Goma, a World Health Organization (WHO) ebola-awareness training session at a hospital was attacked and the doctor deliberately targeted and killed.

However, ebola is not the only challenge the Congolese people face. An estimated one hundred rival militias and the resurgent M23 still roam the eastern provinces of the country looting and pillaging helpless villagers. Even as I write this final chapter at my home in Sydney in June, the villages of the Banyamulenge tribe south of Goma are being attacked and burnt to the ground by local Mai Mai militia, who reject the right of these people to live in Congo because of their link with Rwanda. The longer the inter-tribal and anti-government conflict goes on unresolved the more likely the cycle of retaliation is entrenched, undermining attempts to restore order and build peace. In 2018, film from a place called Maze, site of a recent massacre, made the news in Australia (Fergal Keane, SBS World News, 27 March, 2018). An inconsolable survivor in front of the new graves, where the mounds of freshly turned soil were decorated with sprays of purple bougainvillea, berated the journalist and UN official with him. 'Why do you come making reports of this and yet nothing is done to help us! Who will help us!' he cried in despair. For him, the world looks, then looks away.

Civil unrest simmers despite the elections held last December – two years overdue. The new president is being closely watched as people wait to see how he will handle the rebels suspected of being armed by outside states, and those who smuggle Congo's riches out of the country so that the Congolese people reap no benefit.

***

Given this context and after an absence of two years I was pleased to see signs of some progress as I drove around Goma. Some stretches of road in the centre of town had been kerbed and guttered, and even had footpaths. These areas had been cleared of the pop-up, open-air markets that used to sell everything from plastic buckets and leather sandals to overstuffed velveteen lounge suites. And a zebra crossing had been painted across the road in the busiest part of town. It was, however, a trap for unwary pedestrians: cars and trucks stopped, but the droves of motorcycles, bicycles, *chukudus* and motorised wheelchairs completely ignored it. Parts of the road to Mubambiro had also been sealed so that the drive to the village took less than an hour and was a little easier on my old bones. New buildings had sprung up throughout the city and outer suburbs, which suggested that some people were making a good living, but I feared their prosperity was based on short-term service provision to foreign NGO staff.

Although I hadn't visited for so long, as far as Pygmy Child Care was concerned I'd been very much involved in the management issues that faced our program. In 2018 it became imperative to make changes in the ownership of the Pygmies' land at Mubambiro. When I bought the land for the village in 2011, ten Pygmy men, wise in the ways of the forest and trying to maintain their own values and customs in a different environment, had worked with me. However, Jules, Foro, Sasa, Ferdie and Kamala had all died in recent years. Alexis had often been absent from the village since Cecile, his first wife, had died when overcome by the odourless upwelling of lethal methane gas while gathering edible roots near the forest. And then last year I'd been deeply saddened to learn that Seseti, the patriarch of the village who had led the people out of the forest, had died. Bertin, head of the second extended family group that made up the original village population, was by now elderly and frail. Most of the older women who had grown up in the forest and who had guided me in the design of projects had also died. The deeds for the land were in the names of these men and women who were then heads of households. They'd died leaving no legal wills, so that ownership of the land on which the village was built was open to contest. People still struggled to survive on the informal economy in this area where there was 90 per cent unemployment and no fertile land near enough or secure enough for subsistence farming. No one had savings to pay the land taxes or even to buy essential materials to repair the houses. Consequently, the Good Men held a meeting with everyone in the village in

September 2018 to present a solution to these challenges. With the approval of the villagers, the land was legally registered in the name of Pygmy Child Care. The village was now secured for the children we had been educating, feeding and keeping healthy. I paid the taxes for twenty-five years into the future and provided funds to buy the materials to repair the houses and the community centre.

Last year I also worked with the PCC board to reorganise the management of the agency, employing four professionally qualified and well-recommended people part-time to take on the responsibilities. Fabien was appointed the overall coordinator. Christian replaced Martin as our legal representative when he moved to Beni. Samuel became secretary; Fanny became the accountant; and Thierry, an agronomist, became supplies manager. They have all completed the three-month probationary period and shown themselves to be a competent and committed team.

Christian has also proved to be a courageous and determined advocate for three men from the village who disappeared in June 2018 after telling their families they were planning to go to the forest to pursue traditional survival activities. It was months later that a Bantu man who had disappeared at the same time made it back to Mubambiro and reported that he, along with other Bantu and the three Pygmies, had been arrested and taken hundreds of kilometres away to a military prison. There they were subjected to inhumane conditions and frequent beatings. Christian set off to try to rescue them, accompanied by the devoted mother of one of the men, and Kanari, who said he knew the way to the prison, having been held there himself in the past. After weeks of negotiation and payment of fines that amounted to more than any Pygmy could accumulate in a year, Christian secured the release of two of the men. In dealing with the authorities he was careful not to reveal that the fines were being paid by a foreigner. Instead, he told them that the 'king of the Pygmies' had responded to their need, arguing that God is the king of all, so he was telling the truth. Unfortunately, the third man has been charged with attempting to join a rebel militia in the forest. Although his family and friends insist this was highly unlikely, he remains in captivity. I don't have the resources or the influence to secure his release.

The two men who were freed, Stamani and Muhindu, still traumatised and suffering from malnutrition and maltreatment, are thankful for their rescue. But Stamani has six children and told me he is desperate because he has no other way to support his family than to go back to the forest to hunt and forage. Other people I know also continue to go to the forest to make charcoal, despite the risks. This is a physically exhausting, dangerous and illegal occupation but the only work that offers sufficient income to sustain a family for a few months. They walk the seven kilometres to the nearest entry point to the forest and gather a pile of wood which needs to fire slowly for three days while the wood converts into charcoal. Husband or wife must stay in the forest to guard the fire, but at the same time must hide from rebels, bandits and the government army and forestry patrols. They know of scores of neighbours who have disappeared or been imprisoned like Stamani when discovered in this occupation.

Figure 11.2: Christian with Stamani, the man he rescued from the forest, and three of Stamani's children

While I was in Goma I met with my friend Bishop Desiree, Bishop of North Kivu Diocese, and he promised to use his influence with international donors to fund some farming or small animal husbandry projects in the village. Thierry, Samuel and Christian have met with him to follow up on this but with no result as yet.

Fabien, President of the PCC board, continues to conduct the Child and Maternal Health Clinic in the village and brought two special-needs cases to my attention during my visit. Four-year-old Alex had an umbilical hernia the size of two fists, and mother-of-nine Monique had an enormous goitre which had grown down into her chest and was compressing her heart and dilating important blood vessels. If for no other reason, I was glad I was there to organise life-saving and life-changing surgery for these two people. As it happened, I was staying at Maji Matulivu where I'd stayed on my first visit in 2009. Also staying there for several months was the amazing Australian surgeon Neil Wetzig. He was teaching advanced surgical techniques to the staff at HEAL Africa Hospital. Because the degree of skill and knowledge required for these two cases presented an excellent teaching opportunity for the four Congolese surgeons working with Neil, he was able to arrange for all treatment to be free. Both Alex and Monique have returned to the village with a new lease on life.

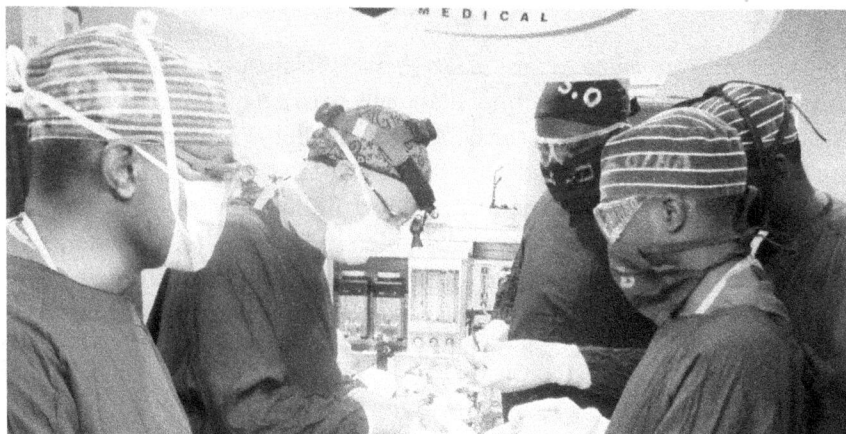

Figure 11.3: Australian surgeon Neil Wetzig and his team at HAH

Figure 11.4: With Dr Jo Lusi at HAH, April 2019

I was warmly welcomed to the village on my arrival, but walking around on the first day back I saw something that really worried me. Funds donated in Australia, New Zealand and the USA through Global Development Group are tax deductible, and any structures built with these funds are required to have signs acknowledging the contribution of these governments. But the signs on the village buildings now read merely: Built with the assistance of the government. It took a while for me to understand that in their effort to emphasise the aid from Australia they had used red paint for the word 'Australian'. They had to demonstrate to convince me that unfortunately this paint wasn't weather-proof and that was why it looked as if all reference to Australia had been removed!

The Palm Sunday service at the centre was a highlight of this visit, with eighty members of the village attending. Many of the women were dressed in what were obviously new clothes, suggesting there was a little more prosperity in the village. When I arrived, Zaina, matriarch of the village, embraced me and pulled me into the welcome dance, which was accompanied by two drums being beaten with such gusto my ears hurt. I had never seen Zaina in such finery and later learnt that her daughter, Natalie, who had completed the sewing classes several years ago, had made it for her in brightly patterned cloth and a stylish design. The Mothers Union Choir, dressed in saffron robes, sang and danced, and the Little Angels Children's Choir sang for us while waving palm fronds in their hands. Faithful Thomson led the service and Revd Joseph from Goma preached with great fervour, at one point commandeering one of the drums to emphasise his enthusiasm.

Figure 11.5: Welcomed back to Mubambiro by Zaina

Figure 11.6: Palm Sunday with the Angels Choir

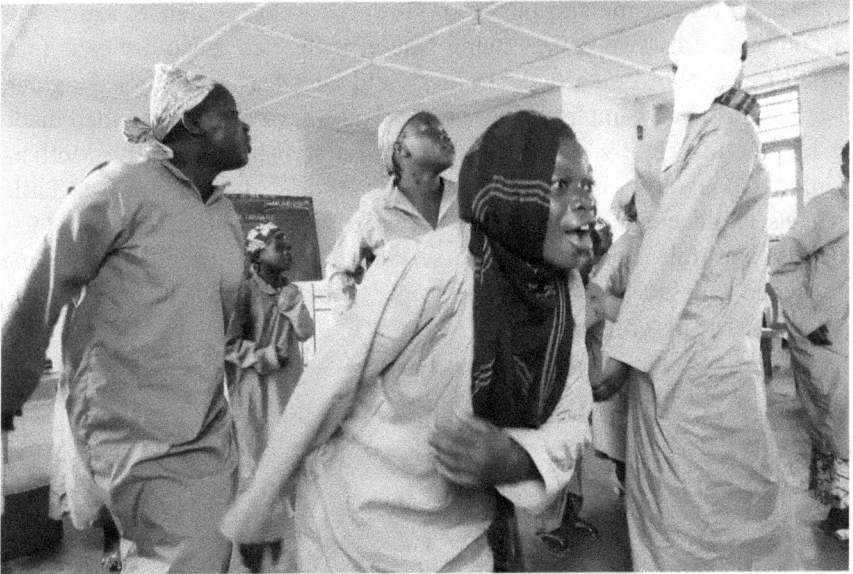

Figure 11.7: The Mothers Union Choir

Nevertheless, for many people in the village and the region, life is still uncertain and difficult beyond our understanding. The widespread, ongoing low-level conflict that rarely makes the news in Australia means 4.6 million people are displaced within Congo and another 746 000 have crossed borders seeking refuge in neighbouring countries. According to a United Nations report (UNOCHA 2018), the increased insecurity of farming in Congo means that thirteen million people desperately need food aid, double the number in need in 2017. Essential public services like education are so reduced that a generation of children are growing up with little or no schooling. Half of the estimated eighty million people in Congo are under fourteen years of age and 4.6 million of these children are critically malnourished. Health services are inadequate and not free, and in 2017–18 the nation had suffered the worst outbreak of cholera in fifteen years.

Sadly, the epidemic of sexual violence continues unchecked in the country once referred to as 'the rape capital of the world' (BBC News 2010) and 'the worst place in the world to be a woman and a mother' (Save the Children 2013). The Nobel Peace Prize this year went to two people, Denis Mukwege and Nadia Murad, for their work to combat the use of sexual violence in war. Dr Mukwege, a Congolese, has dedicated his life to providing specialist care for mutilated rape survivors at the Panzi Hospital, which he founded in Bukavu. He was interviewed for that *Sydney Morning Herald* article back in 2007 that took me to Congo. The honour is well-deserved and for some people in Congo raised hopes that the attention this brings to the suffering of the nation's women might lead to concerted efforts to put an end to the conflict. Unfortunately there are vested interests in maintaining insecurity and a lack of incentive for powerful forces to work for stability.

Some friends can't understand why I've continued to go back and work in the face of the disappointments and the overwhelming needs that have no foreseeable end. In the wider context of international aid, agencies responding to crises around the world are under pressure to move on from providing humanitarian emergency relief to funding only sustainable development programs. That may be possible and desirable in countries with a stable government, but it isn't a reasonable expectation in countries with long-term war and civil strife like Congo. People live with insecurity; life is precarious and the future uncertain. The best-laid plans fail when violence flares up and people must take flight. Traditional values and rules of acceptable behaviour are difficult to maintain in these situations, and even the worst atrocities may be committed with impunity. People must live in the moment, seizing immediate advantages just to survive. Against this background it isn't surprising that aid is sometimes unsuccessful or stolen. Acknowledging the temptations and understanding the compelling personal need that prompts some people to misappropriate aid helps me maintain my commitment to the people at Mubambiro.

Moreover, despite the difficulties the people of Congo face, I have been privileged to meet and work with people who are resilient in the face of setbacks. They seize the opportunities offered them and also contribute to society rather than give in to apathy about the general situation in the country. I'm so encouraged to see people like Evelyn, once a humiliated rape survivor, now a respected, accomplished leader in the village. And Dieudonne, that fatherless little boy who amazed me in 2011 by coming second in his class after just six months in school. Dieudonne has gone on to complete his apprenticeship in motor mechanics, including advanced work with modern computerised vehicles, and on graduating had no trouble finding full employment. When I learnt last year that he had moved to Kitshanga I feared that this would be the last I'd hear of him. But just recently he has been in touch to say he is now an instructor in a technical college. Remembering the help he received to have a better life, he wants to help other children from the village to study with him.

Kayese, one of the first of our high school graduates, has completed his community development studies and has taken on a leadership role with the men. At the Parish Council meeting earlier this year he noted that the Mothers Union within the village has made a difference in the support it provides for the women. Now he has set up a Fathers Union to deal with the problems of alcohol abuse and domestic violence, and to promote 'positive masculinity'. Eric has graduated with the rare distinction of gaining a 65 per cent average score in the State Finals Examinations, and while studying to be a nurse helps Fabien at the monthly clinics. Heritier, Mustafa and Usubi, another child in high school, continue to top their classes at the local high school and promise to provide an educated leadership for the next generation.

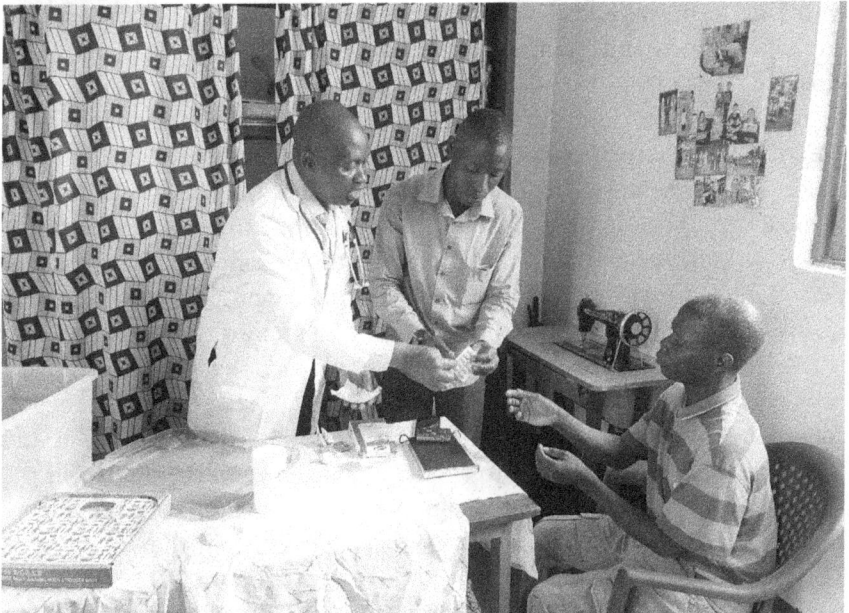

Figure 11.8: Eric, who graduated from high school last year with an exceptional score of 65 per cent, is studying to be a nurse and assisting Fabien at the monthly clinic

Figure 11.9: Heritier, a future leader, topped his classes. Here he is playing the drum for the preschool children

Immensely encouraging also is the success of the program for the youngest children. Despite the truly awful numbers of severely malnourished children in the nation, at Mubambiro we are making a difference in the lives of 138 children under the age of seven. When I first met this group of Pygmies, three out of every ten of the children died before they had turned five years old. None of our children are severely malnourished now. Evelyn and her team continue to provide a program of educational activities, and breakfast and lunch, five days per week for all the children under seven years. Fabien visits once a month to identify and treat minor wounds, coughs, colds and intestinal parasites. He or Evelyn identify children with special needs and finds appropriate treatment for them. All pregnant and breastfeeding women in the Pygmy village have their diet supplemented, and receive ante-natal and post-natal care to prepare them for a good birth, and to make sure their baby thrives. Fourteen of the children continue to study at primary school and three are still in high school.

Even though many adults in the Pygmy village are lucky if they can eat beans and rice a couple of times a week, their children, fed daily and being educated, have the foundation for a better life than their parents have ever dreamed of. None of this could have happened or can continue without the generous and often unexpected support of friends and strangers in Australia and elsewhere. If readers take nothing else from this account of my unique experiences, I hope they will see that it is possible to make a difference for people even while they live under the threat of ongoing conflict in a failed state.

Figure 11.10: Pygmy Child Care provides nutrition, health care, clothing and education for 138 children from some of the poorest families in the world

How to donate to Pygmy Child Care

All donations to Pygmy Child Care should be made through Global Development Group (GDG – ABN 57102400993). The project number for Pygmy Child Care is J893N. GDG is an Australian NGO approved by the Department of Foreign Affairs and Trade. It carries out aid and development activities around the world with approved partners to relieve poverty and provide long-term solutions. Donations to GDG are tax deductible for Australian, US and New Zealand taxpayers.

Donate online: www.gdg.org.au/InfoJ893N

Donate by cheque:
Make your cheque payable to Global Development Group – Project J893N. Please attach a note that the donation is for J893N Pygmy Child Care.

For Australian donors, send your cheque to:
Global Development Group
PO Box 651 Rochedale South
QLD 4123
Australia

Those donating by cheque from other countries should check the GDG website for details.

All royalties from the sale of this book go to Pygmy Child Care through Global Development Group.

Author's note

This book is about my experiences in the Democratic Republic of the Congo (DRC) and in particular my relationship with a specific group of Pygmies as it developed over ten years. My understanding of the people and the country grew over the years, based more on what I learnt in the course of my activities than what I read in published materials. Much of what I say was gained in conversations with my colleagues when we were on the road, or when I asked for clarification of a comment by participants in my seminars for HAH staff or for the Pygmy caregivers, or when I was wandering around the village chatting to people. Congo takes in a vast territory and diverse terrain, and the several hundred tribes have their own languages and customs, so I can't say whether or not what I report here is relevant to other parts of Congo or other groups of Pygmies.

When I sat down to write this book, my observations and the opinions passed on to me by locals and expatriates in Goma were also informed by a scrapbook of cuttings on the situation in Congo from newspapers and journals that interested friends had sent me over the years. The most recent and authoritative was from the *Economist*, 17 February 2018, which featured a photo of a column of soldiers on a Congo street on the cover, and the headline 'Heading back to hell – Congo in peril'.

A primary source of background information in the academic literature was the *Forced Migration Review*, no. 36, November 2010, published by the Refugee Studies Centre at the University of Oxford. This issue of the review was devoted almost entirely to research on the DRC. The article by Baptiste Raymond was particularly relevant.

Theodore Trefon's *Congo Masquerade*, published in 2011, was a most accessible and insightful critique of aid in the DRC. This reliable and valuable reference confirmed much of what I'd learnt about the challenges of making a real difference in the lives of the general population in the country, and particularly in North Kivu province where I worked.

For background on the forest-dwellers known as Pygmies, Colin Turnbull's *The Forest People*, a fascinating account of his two years living in Congo with a group in the forest, first published in 1961, provided a background to understanding the accounts of forest life that the elders at Mubambiro shared with me.

Of all the published materials about Congo that have influenced me over the years, the most crucial was the article by Brian O'Connell in the *Sydney Morning Herald*, weekend edition, 24–25 November 2007. 'The world continues to look away. Don't,' read the headline. I read on, and so began a life-changing journey for me. Brian, if ever you read this, I thank you for being the catalyst for my unmissable experiences in Congo.

Bibliography

BBC News. 'DRC Rape Capital of the World says Margaret Wallstrom, UN special representative on sexual violence in conflict', 28 April 2010.

The Economist. 'Congo – Africa's great war reignites', 17 February 2018, p. 9.

The Economist. 'Congo – Waiting to erupt', Briefing, 17 February 2018, pp.18–22.

Finkel, Michael. 'The Volcano Next Door', *National Geographic*, April 2011, pp. 82–99.

Jenkins, Mark. 'Who murdered the gorillas?', *National Geographic*, June 2008, pp. 34–65.

Keane, Fergal. Report from Maze, DRC, SBS World News, 27 March 2018.

McCallister, P. *PYGMONIA – In Search of the Secret Land of the Pygmies*, University of Queensland Press, St Lucia, 2010.

McLynn, F. *Stanley – The Making of an African Explorer 1841–1877*, Cooper Square Press, New York, 1989.

Meredith, M. *The State of Africa – A History of Fifty Years of Independence*, Free Press, London, 2005.

O'Connell, Brian. 'The world continues to look away. Don't', *Sydney Morning Herald – Weekend Edition*, 24–25 Nov. 2007, p. 29.

Raymond, B. 'Land, IDPs and Mediation', *Forced Migration Review*, no. 36, Nov., Refugee Studies Centre, University of Oxford, 2010. (See also other articles in this edition devoted to the Democratic Republic of the Congo.)

https://blogs.savethechildren.org.uk/2013/05/democratic-republic-of-congo-worst-place-to-be-a-mum/

Save the Children, *State of the World's Mothers 2013*, 7 May 2013

Trefon, T. *Congo Masquerade – The Political Culture of Aid Inefficiency and Reform Failure*, Zed Books, London, 2011.

Turnbull, C. *The Forest People*, Triad/Paladin, Grafton Books, London, 1988.

United Nations Office of Coordination of Humanitarian Affairs (UNOCHA), https://unocha.exposure.co/eight-facts-about-the-humanitarian-crisis-in-the-democratic-republic-of-the-congo.

Vinck, P., Pham, P., Baldo, S. & Shigekhane, R. *Living with Fear – A Population-based Survey on Attitudes about Peace, Justice and Social Reconstruction in Eastern Democratic Republic of Congo*, Human Rights Centre, University of California Berkeley Payton Centre for International Development/Tulane University International Centre for Transitional Justice, August 2008.